The Complete

Breville

Smart Air Fryer Oven Pro

Cookbook with Pictures

Easy-To-Follow & Mouth-Watering Oven Recipes with Exquisite Pictures for Beginners | Assist You to Bake, Roast, Broil, Toast and Make Cookies for Whole Family

Rosemarie Holder

Contents

Introduction

The Breville Smart Oven Air Fryer Pro represents the pinnacle of culinary innovation, combining cutting-edge technology with unmatched versatility. As a marvel of modern kitchen engineering, this appliance redefines the cooking experience, offering a multifunctional solution to elevate every meal. With its sleek design and intuitive interface, the Smart Oven Air Fryer Pro seamlessly integrates into any kitchen, becoming an indispensable tool for home chefs and cooking enthusiasts alike.

Equipped with advanced Element iQ technology, the oven delivers precise and consistent heat distribution, ensuring perfect results every time. Whether you're air frying, roasting, baking, toasting, or dehydrating, this appliance excels in every task, effortlessly accommodating a wide range of cooking needs. Its spacious interior provides ample room for large meals or multiple dishes, while the super convection setting facilitates rapid and even cooking, saving time without compromising on quality.

Beyond its impressive performance, the Smart Oven Air Fryer Pro prioritizes convenience and user-friendliness. Intuitive controls and preprogrammed settings streamline the cooking process, while the inclusion of accessories like air fry baskets and baking pans expands culinary possibilities. This cookbook is your go-to guide for making the most out of your Breville Smart Oven Air Fryer Pro. From crispy appetizers to mouthwatering mains and decadent desserts, each recipe is tailored to showcase the oven's versatility. With easy-to-follow instructions, handy tips, and tempting photos, this cookbook makes gourmet cooking at home a breeze. Elevate your culinary skills and indulge in restaurant-quality meals right from your kitchen. Say hello to convenience and culinary excellence all in one place! From crispy fries to succulent roasts, this appliance empowers users to unleash their culinary creativity and enjoy restaurant-quality results from the comfort of their homes. Experience the future of cooking with the Breville Smart Oven Air Fryer Pro — where innovation meets flavor, and every meal becomes a masterpiece.

Fundamentals of Breville Smart Oven Air Fryer Pro

The Breville Smart Oven Air Fryer Pro is a compact countertop appliance offering multiple cooking functions.

1. Design: Sleek stainless-steel exterior, compact size fits on countertops.

2. Functions: Combines baking, roasting, broiling, toasting, and reheating.

3. Air Frying: Uses convection technology for crispy results with less oil.

4. Convection Cooking: Ensures even cooking throughout.

5. Control: Easy temperature and time adjustment with pre-set programs.

6. Accessories: Includes pizza pan, baking pan, and broil rack.

7. Cleaning: Non-stick interior, removable crumb tray for easy cleaning.

8. Safety: Auto shut-off, cool-touch exterior.

Understanding these basics will maximize your Breville Smart Oven Air Fryer Pro's potential in the kitchen.

What is Breville Smart Oven Air Fryer Pro?

The Breville Smart Oven Air Fryer Pro is a versatile kitchen appliance that combines several cooking functions into one sleek unit. As the name suggests, it's not just an oven but a smart kitchen device with multifunctional capabilities, designed to streamline your cooking process and expand your culinary options.

At its core, the Breville Smart Oven Air Fryer Pro is an oven that offers a variety of cooking methods, including baking, roasting, broiling, toasting, reheating and slow cooking. What sets it apart from traditional ovens and air fryers is its integration of smart technology and a range of convenient features.

One of the standout features of this appliance is its smart functionality, which allows for precise and consistent cooking. Equipped with advanced cooking algorithms, it can automatically adjust time and temperature settings based on the selected cooking function and the type of food being prepared. This takes the guesswork out of cooking and ensures optimal results every time.

It allows you to enjoy the crispy texture of fried foods using significantly less oil compared to traditional frying methods. This not only makes meals healthier but also reduces mess and cleanup time.

In addition to its cooking prowess, the Breville Smart Oven Air Fryer Pro boasts a spacious interior that can accommodate a variety of dishes, from pizzas and casseroles to whole chickens and roasts. It also features multiple cooking racks and trays, allowing you to cook different foods simultaneously without flavors mixing.

The appliance is designed with user convenience in mind, featuring an intuitive control panel with easy-to-read displays and preset cooking

functions for popular dishes. It also comes with accessories such as a pizza pan, baking pan, and broil rack, providing everything you need to start cooking right out of the box.

Overall, the Breville Smart Oven Air Fryer Pro is a versatile and efficient kitchen appliance that offers the convenience of multiple cooking methods in a single unit. Whether you're looking to broil, bake, roast, or toast, this appliance has you covered, making it a valuable addition to any kitchen.

Benefits of Using It

The Breville Smart Oven Air Fryer Pro is a multifunctional kitchen appliance that combines the functions of a conventional oven, an air fryer, and several other cooking appliances into one compact unit. Here are some of the benefits of using the Breville Smart Oven Air Fryer Pro:

1. Versatility: This appliance offers a wide range of cooking functions, including baking, roasting, broiling, toasting, reheating and more. This versatility allows you to prepare a variety of dishes without needing multiple appliances, saving both space and time in the kitchen.

2. Healthier Cooking: The air frying function uses significantly less oil compared to traditional deep frying methods, resulting in healthier meals with less fat and fewer calories. It allows you to enjoy crispy and delicious fried foods with a fraction of the oil, making it a great option for those looking to reduce their fat intake.

3. Convenient Size: The Breville Smart Oven Air Fryer Pro is designed to be compact yet spacious enough to accommodate a variety of dishes. It's ideal for small kitchens or for those who don't have space for a full-sized oven. Despite its smaller footprint, it can still handle cooking tasks typically reserved for larger appliances.

4. Precision Cooking: With advanced features such as Element IQ technology, this appliance delivers precise and consistent cooking results. It automatically adjusts the cooking time and temperature based on the selected function and food type, ensuring that your meals are cooked to perfection every time.

5. Time-Saving: The Breville Smart Oven Air Fryer Pro preheats faster than a conventional oven, allowing you to start cooking your meals more quickly. Additionally, its convection cooking feature ensures even heat distribution, reducing cooking times and helping you get dinner on the table faster.

6. Easy to Clean: The appliance features a nonstick interior coating and removable crumb tray, making it easy to clean up after cooking. Many of its accessories, such as the broiling rack and baking pan, are also dishwasher safe, further simplifying the cleaning process.

7. Energy Efficiency: Compared to a traditional oven, the Breville

Smart Oven Air Fryer Pro consumes less energy, helping you save on utility bills while still enjoying the convenience of a full-featured cooking appliance.

8. Intuitive Controls: The appliance features easy-to-use digital controls and an LCD, making it simple to select the desired cooking function, time, and temperature. It also offers preset cooking programs for popular dishes, further streamlining the cooking process.

Overall, the Breville Smart Oven Air Fryer Pro is a versatile and efficient kitchen appliance that offers a wide range of cooking functions, making it a valuable addition to any kitchen. Whether you're looking to air fry crispy snacks, bake homemade bread, or roast a succulent chicken, this appliance delivers consistent results with ease.

Quick Start Guide

To ensure proper oven setup and performance:
1. Remove all protective substances by running the oven empty for 15 minutes, ensuring proper ventilation.
2. Safely discard packing material, labels, and tape.
3. Wash accessories thoroughly with warm, soapy water and dry them completely.
4. Wipe the interior of the oven and place it on a flat, dry surface with ample space around it.
5. Insert the crumb tray.
6. Unwind the power cord and plug it into a grounded outlet.
7. The oven will alert and display function options on the LCD screen.
8. Rotate the function dial to select the desired function, such as PIZZA.
9. Press the START/CANCEL button to initiate preheating.
10. Once preheated, the temperature alert will sound, indicating readiness.
11. The timer will automatically start counting down once cooking begins.
12. At the end of the cycle, the oven alert will sound, and the LCD screen will change color.
13. The oven is now ready for use.

Step-By-Step Using Breville Smart Oven Air Fryer Pro

1. Insert the wire rack with spokes facing upward into the desired position. Rack positions are indicated on the right side of the oven door window.
2. Turn the FUNCTION dial until the indicator aligns with the desired setting on the LCD screen.
3. Adjust the cooking temperature by rotating the TEMPERATURE dial left to reduce or right to increase. The top figure on the LCD screen indicates the preset temperature or darkness level for the TOAST and BAGEL settings.
4. Adjust the cooking time by rotating the TIME dial left to decrease or right to increase. The bottom figure on the LCD screen indicates preset time or pizza size for the PIZZA setting.
5. For settings without a preheat cycle (TOAST, BAGEL, BROIL, REHEAT, WARM), place food directly on the wire rack or included pizza pan, broiling rack, and/or baking pan. Ensure food is centered for even cooking:
   a) Close the oven door.
   b) Press the START/CANCEL button, illuminating red.
   c) The timer displays and counts down, allowing adjustments to

temperature and time during the cycle.
6. At the commencement of a preheat cycle (BAKE, ROAST, PIZZA, COOKIES, SLOW COOK), engage the START/CANCEL button before placing food in the oven. The button's red backlight will glow, the oven will emit an alert, and the LCD screen will display a blinking 'PREHEATING' as the oven warms up.
   a) Once the oven reaches readiness, the blinking 'PREHEATING' will cease, accompanied by an alert, and the timer will commence counting down. Introduce the food onto the wire rack or the provided pizza pan, broiling rack, and/or baking pan, ensuring it is centrally positioned for even cooking.
   b) Shut the oven door securely.
   c) The timer will persist in its countdown. Adjustments to cooking temperature and time can be made during the cooking process.

Upon completion of the cooking cycle, the oven will emit an alert, the START/CANCEL button's backlight will extinguish, and the LCD screen will emit a blue light.

Toast Function

1. Insert the wire rack into the middle rack height position, with the spokes facing upward.
2. Center 1-3 slices or evenly space 4-6 slices on the wire rack.
3. Close the oven door securely.
4. Turn the FUNCTION dial to select the TOAST function on the LCD screen.
5. Adjust the darkness setting and number of slices as desired:
   a) Turn the TEMPERATURE dial to adjust the darkness setting.
   b) Turn the TIME dial to adjust the number of slices.
6. Press the START/CANCEL button to initiate the TOAST function; the button backlight will turn red, the oven alert will sound, and the LCD screen will illuminate orange.
7. The timer will start counting down automatically; adjust the time as needed during the cycle by turning the TIME dial, and stop the cycle at any time by pressing the START/CANCEL button.
8. At the end of the TOAST cycle, the oven alert will sound; the START/CANCEL button backlight will turn off, and the LCD screen will illuminate blue.

Bagel Function

1. Insert the wire rack, with the spokes facing upward, into the middle rack height position.
2. If toasting 1–3 bagel halves, center the slices on the wire rack. If toasting 4–6 halves, evenly space them with 2–3 halves at the front of the wire rack and 2–3 halves at the back of the rack.
3. Close the oven door.
4. Turn the FUNCTION dial until the indicator on the LCD screen reaches the BAGEL function. The top figure on the LCD screen indicates the preset darkness setting '4', while the bottom figure indicates the preset number of bagel halves '4'.
5. The darkness setting and number of bagel halves can be adjusted before or during the toasting cycle.
   a) The darkness level is shown by the row of triangles on the LCD screen's top. To adjust the darkness, turn the TEMPERATURE dial left to decrease it or right to increase it. The circle beneath the triangles will shift based on the setting chosen. As a general guide:

DESIRED BAGEL COLOR SETTING

Light 1 or 2
Medium 3, 4, or 5
Dark 6 or 7

b) The number of bagel halves is displayed as the bottom figure on the LCD screen. Turn the TIME dial to the left to reduce the number of bagel halves, or to the right to increase it. The number of bagel halves ranges from '1' to '6'.

6. Activate the BAGEL function by pressing the START/CANCEL button. The backlight of the button will turn red, the oven will beep, and the LCD screen will light up in orange.

7. The timer will appear and start counting down automatically. You can modify the time by turning the TIME dial during the bagel cycle. Press the START/CANCEL button at any time to stop the cycle.

8. When the BAGEL cycle finishes, the oven will beep again. The backlight of the START/CANCEL button will turn off, and the LCD screen will change to a blue illumination.

Bake Function

1. The BAKE function evenly cooks food throughout. Ideal for baking cakes, muffins, brownies, and pastries. Also perfect for cooking prepackaged frozen meals like lasagna and pot pies.

2. Insert the wire rack with spokes facing upward into the bottom rack height position. Note that certain baked goods, such as brownies or pastries, may suit the middle rack height position better.

3. Close the oven door.

4. Turn the FUNCTION dial until the indicator on the LCD screen reaches the BAKE function. The top figure on the LCD screen indicates the preset BAKE temperature of '325°F', while the bottom figure indicates the preset time of ':30 MINS'. The preset CONVECTION setting will also be displayed.

5. The temperature and duration of the baking process can be modified both before and during the cycle. a) The baking temperature appears at the top of the LCD screen. Adjust it between 120°F/50°C and 450°F/230°C using the TEMPERATURE dial.
   b) The baking time is shown at the bottom of the LCD screen. Use the TIME dial to set it for up to 2 hours at temperatures above 300°F/150°C, or up to 10 hours for temperatures below 300°F/150°C.

6. Initiate the BAKE function by pressing the START/CANCEL button. The backlight of the button will glow red, an oven alert will sound, and the LCD screen will light up in orange with a 'PREHEATING' indicator flashing.

7. An alert will sound once the oven reaches the desired temperature.

8. Position food in the center of the wire rack using the provided baking pan or another oven-proof dish to ensure airflow around all sides.

9. The timer will start counting down automatically after the PREHEATING alert. Adjust the temperature and time as needed during baking by turning the TEMPERATURE and TIME dials. To halt the cycle at any point, press the START/CANCEL button.

10. At the conclusion of the BAKE cycle, the oven will alert you, the START/CANCEL button's backlight will turn off, and the LCD screen will display a blue light.

Roast Function

1. Insert the wire rack with spokes facing upward into the bottom rack height position.

2. Close the oven door.

3. Turn the FUNCTION dial until the LCD screen indicator aligns with the ROAST function. The top figure indicates the preset ROAST temperature of '350°F', while the bottom figure shows the preset time of '1:00HRS'. The preset CONVECTION setting is also displayed.

4. Adjust the roasting temperature and time before or during the cycle.
   a) Turn the TEMPERATURE dial to set the baking temperature from 120°F/50°C to a maximum of 450°F/230°C.
   b) Use the TIME dial to select up to 2 hours for temperatures above 300°F/150°C and up to 10 hours for temperatures below 300°F/150°C.

5. Press the START/CANCEL button to activate the ROAST function. The button backlight turns red, the oven alert sounds, and the

LCD screen illuminates orange with a blinking 'PREHEATING' indication.

6. Once the oven reaches the set temperature, the temperature alert sounds.

7. Place food on the included baking pan or another oven-proof dish, positioned at the center of the wire rack to ensure even airflow around all sides.

8. After the PREHEATING alert, the timer automatically begins counting down. Adjust temperature and time using the corresponding dials during the cycle. Press the START/CANCEL button to stop the cycle at any time.

9. At the end of the ROAST cycle, the oven alert sounds, the START/CANCEL button backlight turns off, and the LCD screen illuminates blue.

Broil Function

1. Insert the wire rack, with the spokes facing upward, into the top rack height position.

2. Insert the included broiling rack into the baking pan.

3. Place food on the assembled broiling rack or in an oven-proof dish, then place on the center of the wire rack so air flows around the sides of the food.

4. Turn the FUNCTION dial until the indicator on the LCD screen reaches the BROIL function.

5. The top figure on the LCD screen indicates the preset temperature of '500°F', while the bottom figure indicates the preset time of ':10 MINS'.

6. Press the START/CANCEL button to activate the BROIL function.

7. The button backlight will illuminate red, the oven alert will sound, and the LCD screen will illuminate orange.

8. The broiling temperature and time can be adjusted before or during the broiling cycle.
   a) The broiling temperature is displayed as the top figure on the LCD screen. Turn the TEMPERATURE dial to adjust broiling to one of three pre-set temperatures: 500°F, 400°F, 300°F.
   b) The broiling time is displayed as the bottom figure on the LCD screen. Turn the TIME dial to adjust the time up to 20 minutes.

9. The timer will be displayed and automatically begin to count down.

10. The temperature and time can be adjusted during the broiling cycle by turning the corresponding TEMPERATURE and TIME dials.

11. The cycle can be stopped at any time by pressing the START/CANCEL button.

12. At the end of the BROIL cycle, the oven alert will sound.

13. The START/CANCEL button backlight will go out, and the LCD screen will illuminate blue.

Pizza Function

1. To activate the PIZZA function:
   a) Insert the wire rack into the middle rack height position, with the spokes facing upward.
   b) Close the oven door securely.
   c) Turn the FUNCTION dial until the indicator on the LCD screen aligns with the PIZZA function. The LCD screen will display the preset temperature of '450°F' and the preset size of 12". Additionally, the preset CONVECTION and FROZEN settings will be shown.

2. Adjustments can be made before or during the cycle:
   a) To adjust the pizza temperature, turn the TEMPERATURE dial. The temperature range is from 120°F/50°C to a maximum of 450°F/230°C.
   b) To modify the pizza size, turn the TIME dial. Sizes range from 6" to 13".

3. Press the START/CANCEL button to initiate the PIZZA function. The button backlight will turn red, an oven alert will sound, and the LCD screen will illuminate orange with a blinking 'PREHEATING' message.

4. Once the oven reaches the set temperature, a temperature alert will sound.

5. Place the food on the included pizza pan in the center of the wire rack, ensuring proper air circulation around all sides.

6. After the PREHEATING alert, the timer will begin counting down automatically. Both temperature and time can be adjusted during the

cycle using the corresponding dials. The cycle can be stopped at any point by pressing the START/CANCEL button.

7. At the end of the PIZZA cycle, the oven alert will sound again. The START/CANCEL button backlight will turn off, and the LCD screen will illuminate blue.

Cookies Function

1. The COOKIES function is perfect for baking homemade or commercially prepared cookies and other baked treats, including ready-to-bake crescent rolls, cinnamon scrolls, biscuits, and strudels.
2. Close the oven door, then insert the wire rack into the middle rack height position, ensuring the spokes face upward.
3. Turn the FUNCTION dial until the COOKIES function indicator aligns with the indicator on the LCD screen. The top figure on the screen denotes the preset temperature of '350°F', while the bottom figure indicates the preset time of ':11 MINS'. The preset CONVECTION setting is also displayed.
4. Adjust the baking temperature and time as needed before or during the cookie cycle:
   a) The baking temperature is shown as the top figure on the LCD screen. Turn the TEMPERATURE dial to adjust it from 120°F/50°C to a maximum of 450°F/230°C.
   b) The baking time is displayed as the bottom figure on the LCD screen. Turn the TIME dial to set it for up to 1 hour.
5. Activate the COOKIES function by pressing the START/CANCEL button. The button backlight will turn red, the oven alert will sound, and the LCD screen will illuminate orange with a blinking 'PREHEATING' indication.
6. Once the oven reaches the set temperature, the temperature alert will sound.
7. Position food, placed on the included baking pan, pizza pan, or other oven-proof dish, at the center of the wire rack to ensure even airflow around all sides of the food.
8. After the PREHEATING alert, the timer will automatically start counting down. Adjust the temperature and time during the cycle using the corresponding TEMPERATURE and TIME dials. You can stop the cycle at any point by pressing the START/CANCEL button.
9. When the COOKIES cycle ends, the oven alert will sound. The backlight of the START/CANCEL button will extinguish, and the LCD screen will illuminate blue.

Reheat Function

1. Insert the wire rack into the bottom rack height position, with the spokes facing upward.
2. Place food on the center of the wire rack, using the included baking pan, pizza pan, or another ovenproof dish, ensuring airflow around all sides.
3. Close the oven door securely.
4. Turn the FUNCTION dial until the indicator reaches the REHEAT function on the LCD screen. The top figure indicates the preset temperature of '325°F', while the bottom figure shows the preset time of ':15 MINS'. The preset CONVECTION setting is also displayed.
5. Adjust the reheating temperature and time as needed:
   a) Turn the TEMPERATURE dial to set the temperature from 120°F/50°C to a maximum of 450°F/230°C (displayed as the top figure).

b) Turn the TIME dial to adjust the time up to 2 hours (displayed as the bottom figure).
6. Press the START/CANCEL button to activate the REHEAT function. The button backlight will turn red, the oven alert will sound, and the LCD screen will illuminate orange.
7. The timer will begin to count down and be displayed. Adjust temperature and time during the cycle by turning the corresponding dials. Press START/CANCEL to stop the cycle at any time.
8. At the end of the REHEAT cycle, the oven alert will sound. The START/CANCEL button backlight will extinguish, and the LCD screen will illuminate blue.

Warm Function

1. The WARM function maintains hot foods at the recommended temperature to prevent bacterial growth (160°F/70°C or above).
2. Insert the wire rack, with the spokes facing upward, into the bottom rack height position.
3. Place food, positioned on the included baking pan, pizza pan, or other oven-proof dish, on the center of the wire rack so air will flow around all sides of the food.
4. Close the oven door.
5. Turn the FUNCTION dial until the indicator on the LCD screen reaches the WARM function. The top figure on the LCD screen indicates the preset temperature of '160°F', while the bottom figure indicates the preset time of '1:00 HRS'. The preset KEEP WARM symbol will also be displayed.
6. You can modify the warming temperature and duration either before or during the warming cycle.
   a) The temperature is shown at the top of the LCD screen. Use the TEMPERATURE dial to set it anywhere from 120°F/50°C to 450°F/230°C.
   b) The time is indicated at the bottom of the LCD screen. Adjust it by turning the TIME dial, setting it for up to 2 hours.
7. To start the WARM function, press the START/CANCEL button. This will make the button's backlight turn red, trigger an oven alert, and cause the LCD screen to light up orange.
8. The timer will appear and start to count down automatically. You can adjust both the temperature and time during the warming cycle by using the TEMPERATURE and TIME dials. You can stop the cycle anytime by pressing the START/CANCEL button.
9. When the WARM cycle concludes, the oven will beep, the START/CANCEL button's backlight will turn off, and the LCD screen will turn blue.

Slow Cook Function

1. Close the oven door.
2. Insert the wire rack, with the spokes facing upward, into the bottom rack height position.
3. Turn the FUNCTION dial until the indicator on the LCD screen reaches the SLOW COOK function.
4. The LCD screen's top figure displays the default SLOW COOK setting of 'HI', and the bottom figure shows a preset time of '4:00HRS'.
5. Adjustments can be made to the slow cook setting and time:
   a) The slow cook setting, shown as the top figure on the LCD, can be adjusted by turning the TEMPERATURE dial to select either 'LO' or 'HI'.

b) The time, displayed as the bottom figure on the LCD, can be set between 4 and 10 hours for 'LO' and between 2 and 8 hours for 'HI' by turning the TIME dial.

6. Activate the SLOW COOK function by pressing the START/ CANCEL button. The button's backlight will turn red, an oven alert will sound, and the LCD screen will glow orange, indicating 'PREHEATING' is blinking.

7. A temperature alert will sound once the oven reaches the selected temperature.

8. Position food in oven-proof cookware at the center of the wire rack to ensure air circulates around all sides.

9. The timer will start counting down automatically after the PREHEATING alert. During the slow cook cycle, the time can be adjusted by turning the TIME dial, and the cycle can be stopped at any time by pressing the START/CANCEL button.

10. Following the SLOW COOK cycle, the oven will switch automatically to the WARM function. The LCD screen will show 'KEEP WARM', and a countdown from a maximum of '2:00 HRS' will start. This keep-warm cycle can also be stopped anytime by pressing the START/CANCEL button.

Cleaning and Caring for Breville Smart Oven Air Fryer Pro

Cleaning and caring for your Breville Smart Oven Air Fryer Pro is essential for maintaining its performance and prolonging its lifespan.

1. Regular Cleaning:

After each use, allow the oven to cool down completely before cleaning.

Remove the accessories such as the broiling rack, baking pan, and wire rack.

Wipe the interior and exterior surfaces of the oven with a damp cloth or sponge. You can use a mild detergent if needed, but make sure to rinse thoroughly and dry with a clean cloth.

For stubborn stains or grease buildup, you can use a nonabrasive cleaner or a mixture of baking soda and water. Apply the cleaner, let it sit for a few minutes, then wipe clean.

2. Cleaning Accessories:

Wash the air fry basket, baking pan, and wire rack with warm soapy water after each use. Use a sponge or soft brush to remove any food residue.

For tough, baked-on stains, you can soak the accessories in warm, soapy water before cleaning.

Dry the accessories thoroughly before placing them back in the oven.

3. Cleaning the Interior:

Regularly remove crumbs and debris from the interior of the oven using a soft brush or cloth. For thorough cleaning, use the included crumb tray.

Remove it from the oven and discard any crumbs. Wash the crumb tray with warm, soapy water and dry it thoroughly before replacing it.

4. Cleaning the Exterior:

Wipe the exterior surfaces of the oven with a damp cloth to remove any spills or stains.

Avoid using abrasive cleaners or scouring pads, as they may damage the finish of the oven.

For stainless steel surfaces, you can use a stainless steel cleaner to restore shine and remove fingerprints.

5. Cleaning the Heating Elements:

Periodically check the heating elements for any food buildup or residue.

Allow the oven to cool completely, then gently wipe the heating elements with a damp cloth or sponge.

Avoid using abrasive cleaners or scrubbing the heating elements, as this can damage them.

6. Maintenance Tips:

Regularly inspect the power cord for any damage or fraying. If you notice any issues, discontinue use and contact Breville customer service for assistance.

Avoid using harsh chemicals or abrasive materials on any part of the oven, as this can cause damage.

Follow the manufacturer's instructions for any troubleshooting or maintenance procedures.

Frequently Asked Questions & Notes

The oven is not turning on.

• Ensure the power plug is firmly inserted into the outlet.
• Try plugging the oven into a different outlet.
• If available, use an independent outlet.
• Reset the circuit breaker if needed.

I'd like to reset the oven's LCD to its default settings.

By default, the oven remembers the last setting used for each function until you unplug it from the power outlet. To reset the oven's default settings for each function, simply unplug it from the power outlet, wait for 5 seconds, and then plug it back in.

The LCD light is off

The oven enters standby mode if it remains unused for 10 minutes. In this mode, the LCD screen stops lighting up, but all function options remain visible.

To reactivate the oven from standby mode, press the START/CANCEL button or turn any dial, and the LCD screen will light up again.

The pizza cooks unevenly

In compact ovens, large pizzas may not brown evenly. To achieve more uniform cooking, open the oven door mid-way through the bake time and rotate the pizza by 90 degrees.

The Magnetic Auto-Rack Eject extends too far

When opening the oven door, do so slowly and carefully, especially when the wire rack is set at the middle height, to prevent it from ejecting too quickly.

I can't select the FROZEN FOODS button

The FROZEN FOODS button can only be used with the TOAST, BAGEL, PIZZA, and COOKIES settings.

Steam is escaping from the top of the oven door

This is expected behavior. The door is designed to vent steam from cooking high-moisture foods like frozen bread.

The heating elements are flickering

This is normal and part of the Element IQ‰ system, which manages the oven's heat by intermittently powering the heating elements.

Water is leaking onto the counter from the oven door

This is a normal occurrence. Condensation from cooking high-moisture foods can collect and drip down from the inside of the door onto the counter.

4-Week Meal Plan

Week 1

Day 1:
Breakfast: Cheese Cauliflower Hash Browns
Lunch: Spinach, Artichoke & Cauliflower Casserole
Snack: Garlic Butter Cheese Breadsticks
Dinner: Delicious Chicken Enchiladas
Dessert: Perfect Chocolate Mayo Cake

Day 2:
Breakfast: Fluffy Lemon Poppy Seed Cake
Lunch: Mushroom Quesadilla
Snack: Keto Cauliflower Tots
Dinner: Lemony Garlic Shrimp
Dessert: Sweet Cream Puffs

Day 3:
Breakfast: Cinnamon Cheese Bread Sticks
Lunch: Classic Eggplant Lasagna
Snack: Homemade Bruschetta
Dinner: Pork Tenderloin with Avocado Lime Sauce
Dessert: Vanilla Peanut Butter Cookies

Day 4:
Breakfast: Easy Baked "Hard-Boiled" Eggs
Lunch: Cheese Zucchini Tart
Snack: Crispy Onion Rings
Dinner: Cheese Spinach Stuffed Chicken Breast
Dessert: Chocolate Chip Cookies

Day 5:
Breakfast: Sausage Egg & Cheese Breakfast Calzone
Lunch: Crispy Broccoli-Cheese Fritters
Snack: Balsamic Brussels Sprouts with Bacon
Dinner: Fish Sticks with Tartar Sauce
Dessert: Crispy Peanut Butter Cookies

Day 6:
Breakfast: Cheese Sausage Balls
Lunch: Crispy Tofu with Sesame Seeds
Snack: Prosciutto-Wrapped Asparagus
Dinner: Barbecued Pork Riblets
Dessert: Yummy Double Chocolate Brownies

Day 7:
Breakfast: Breakfast Spaghetti Squash Fritters
Lunch: Roasted Brussels Sprouts with Pecans
Snack: Cheese Bacon Stuffed Sweet Peppers
Dinner: Perfect Greek Meatballs with Tzatziki Sauce
Dessert: Cinnamon Cupcakes with Cream Cheese Frosting

Week 2

Day 1:
Breakfast: Cheesy Scrambled Eggs
Lunch: Cheese Zucchini Fritters
Snack: Sausage-Stuffed Peppers
Dinner: Crispy Spicy Chicken Breasts
Dessert: Rich Chocolate Cake

Day 2:
Breakfast: Easy Homemade Cake
Lunch: Savory Buttered Mushrooms
Snack: Delicious Mozzarella Sticks
Dinner: Crispy Coconut Shrimp
Dessert: Cirtus Doughnut Bites

Day 3:
Breakfast: Breakfast Blueberry Muffins
Lunch: Spicy Roasted Bok Choy with Sesame Seeds
Snack: Crispy Cajun-Spiced Kale Chips
Dinner: Spicy Baby Back Ribs
Dessert: Crispy Chocolate–Pecan Biscotti

Day 4:
Breakfast: Homemade Biscuits
Lunch: Roasted Buttered Asparagus
Snack: Spicy Chicken Wings
Dinner: Delicious Chicken Fajitas
Dessert: Fluffy Almond Flour Cinnamon Rolls

Day 5:
Breakfast: Breakfast Egg Pizza
Lunch: Provencal Tomatoes
Snack: Parmesan Zucchini Fries
Dinner: Tuna Patties with Spicy Sriracha Sauce
Dessert: Sweet Chocolate Soufflés

Day 6:
Breakfast: Ham Egg Cups
Lunch: Simple Caramelized Broccoli
Snack: Parmesan Zucchini Chips
Dinner: Beef and Broccoli Stir-Fry
Dessert: Crispy Caramel Apple Crumble

Day 7:
Breakfast: Broccoli Frittata
Lunch: Tasty Roasted Curry Cauliflower
Snack: Roasted Sweet & Spicy Pecans
Dinner: Low-Carb Spaghetti Zoodles and Meatballs
Dessert: Yummy Molten Chocolate Almond Cakes

Week 3

Day 1:
Breakfast: Classic Pancake
Lunch: Spinach, Artichoke & Cauliflower Casserole
Snack: Traditional Scotch Eggs
Dinner: Homemade Rotisserie Chicken
Dessert: Sweet Cream Puffs

Day 2:
Breakfast: Smoky Pork Patties
Lunch: Mushroom Quesadilla
Snack: Flavorful Stuffed Peppers
Dinner: Sweet and Spicy Salmon Fillets
Dessert: Vanilla Peanut Butter Cookies

Day 3:
Breakfast: Spinach-Bacon Egg Muffins
Lunch: Savory Roasted Broccoli with Sesame Dressing
Snack: Keto Cauliflower Tots
Dinner: Tender Peppercorn-Crusted Beef Tenderloin
Dessert: Perfect Chocolate Mayo Cake

Day 4:
Breakfast: Fluffy Lemon Poppy Seed Cake
Lunch: Classic Eggplant Lasagna
Snack: Crispy Onion Rings
Dinner: Classic Chicken Cordon Bleu
Dessert: Yummy Double Chocolate Brownies

Day 5:
Breakfast: Cheesy Scrambled Eggs
Lunch: Cheese Zucchini Tart
Snack: Garlic Butter Cheese Breadsticks
Dinner: Fish Street Tacos with Sriracha Slaw
Dessert: Chocolate Chip Cookies

Day 6:
Breakfast: Crustless Cheese Spinach Frittata
Lunch: Crispy Broccoli-Cheese Fritters
Snack: Balsamic Brussels Sprouts with Bacon
Dinner: Mouthwatering Lasagna Casserole
Dessert: Cinnamon Cupcakes with Cream Cheese Frosting

Day 7:
Breakfast: Breakfast Spaghetti Squash Fritters
Lunch: Crispy Tofu with Sesame Seeds
Snack: Homemade Bruschetta
Dinner: Herbed Garlic Flank Steak
Dessert: Crispy Peanut Butter Cookies

Week 4

Day 1:
Breakfast: Ham Egg Cups
Lunch: Cheese Zucchini Fritters
Snack: Prosciutto-Wrapped Asparagus
Dinner: Delicious Turkey Meatballs
Dessert: Rich Chocolate Cake

Day 2:
Breakfast: Breakfast Egg Pizza
Lunch: Savory Buttered Mushrooms
Snack: Cheese Bacon Stuffed Sweet Peppers
Dinner: Homemade Bang Bang Shrimp
Dessert: Cirtus Doughnut Bites

Day 3:
Breakfast: Breakfast Blueberry Muffins
Lunch: Roasted Buttered Asparagus
Snack: Spicy Chicken Wings
Dinner: Hearty Cheeseburger Casserole
Dessert: Crispy Chocolate–Pecan Biscotti

Day 4:
Breakfast: Homemade Biscuits
Lunch: Tasty Roasted Curry Cauliflower
Snack: Crispy Cajun-Spiced Kale Chips
Dinner: Healthy Spinach and Feta Stuffed Chicken Breasts
Dessert: Fluffy Almond Flour Cinnamon Rolls

Day 5:
Breakfast: Crustless Cheese Spinach Frittata
Lunch: Simple Caramelized Broccoli
Snack: Delicious Mozzarella Sticks
Dinner: Easy Ginger-Scallion Fish
Dessert: Sweet Chocolate Soufflés

Day 6:
Breakfast: Smoky Pork Patties
Lunch: Provencal Tomatoes
Snack: Sausage-Stuffed Peppers
Dinner: Healthy Steak Salad with Smoky Blue Cheese Dressing
Dessert: Crispy Caramel Apple Crumble

Day 7:
Breakfast: Classic Pancake
Lunch: Savory Roasted Broccoli with Sesame Dressing
Snack: Parmesan Zucchini Fries
Dinner: Tasty Bacon Guacamole Burgers
Dessert: Yummy Molten Chocolate Almond Cakes

Fluffy Lemon Poppy Seed Cake

⏱ **Prep: 10 minutes**   🍲 **Cook: 14 minutes**   🍃 **Serves: 6**

Ingredients:

1 cup blanched finely ground almond flour
½ cup powdered erythritol
½ teaspoon baking powder
¼ cup unsalted butter, melted
¼ cup unsweetened almond milk
2 large eggs
1 teaspoon vanilla extract
1 medium lemon
1 teaspoon poppy seeds

Preparation:

1. In a large bowl, mix almond flour, erythritol, baking powder, butter, almond milk, eggs, and vanilla. 2. Slice the lemon in half and squeeze the juice into a small bowl, then add to the batter. 3. Using a fine grater, zest the lemon and add 1 tablespoon zest to the batter and stir. Add poppy seeds to batter. 4. Pour batter into nonstick 6" round cake pan. Insert the wire rack into the middle rack height position. 5. Close the oven door. Turn the FUNCTION dial until the indicator on the LCD screen reaches the BAKE function. Set the temperature to 300°F and set the timer to 14 minutes. Press START/CANCEL to activate. 6. When preheating has completed, place the cake pan on the wire rack and bake for 14 minutes. 7. When fully cooked, a toothpick inserted in center will come out mostly clean. The cake will finish cooking and firm up as it cools. Serve at room temperature.

Per Serving: Calories 141; Fat 10.2g; Sodium 36mg; Carbs 9.33g; Fiber 3.9g; Sugar 1.37g; Protein 7.25g

Easy Homemade Cake

⏱ **Prep: 10 minutes**   🍲 **Cook: 7 minutes**   🍃 **Serves: 4**

Ingredients:

½ cup blanched finely ground almond flour
¼ cup powdered erythritol
½ teaspoon baking powder
2 tablespoons unsalted butter, softened
1 large egg
½ teaspoon unflavored gelatin
½ teaspoon vanilla extract
½ teaspoon ground cinnamon

Preparation:

1. In a large bowl, mix almond flour, erythritol, and baking powder. Add butter, egg, gelatin, vanilla, and cinnamon. Pour into 6" round baking pan. 2. Insert the wire rack into the middle rack height position. Close the oven door. Turn the FUNCTION dial until the indicator on the LCD screen reaches the BAKE function. Set the temperature to 300°F and set the timer to 7 minutes. Press START/CANCEL to activate. 3. When preheating has completed, place the cake pan on the wire rack and bake for 7 minutes. 4. When the cake is completely cooked, a toothpick will come out clean. Cut cake into four and serve.

Per Serving: Calories 93; Fat 5.8g; Sodium 36mg; Carbs 6.55g; Fiber 3g; Sugar 0.93g; Protein 6.71g

Cheese Cauliflower Hash Browns

⏱ Prep: 20 minutes 🍲 Cook: 12 minutes ❧ Serves: 4

Ingredients:

1 (12-ounce) steamer bag cauliflower
1 large egg
1 cup shredded sharp Cheddar cheese

Preparation:

1. Place bag in microwave and cook according to package instructions. Allow to cool completely and put cauliflower into a kitchen towel or cheesecloth and squeeze to remove excess moisture. 2. Mash cauliflower with a fork and add egg and cheese. 3. Cut a piece of parchment to fit your baking pan. Take ¼ of the mixture and form it into a hash brown patty shape. Place it onto the parchment and into the baking pan, working in batches if necessary. 4. Insert the wire rack into the middle rack height position. Close the oven door. Turn the FUNCTION dial until the indicator on the LCD screen reaches the BAKE function. Set the temperature to 400°F and set the timer to 12 minutes. Press START/CANCEL to activate. 5. When preheating has completed, place the baking pan on the wire rack and bake for 12 minutes. 6. Flip the hash browns halfway through the cooking time. When completely cooked, they will be golden brown. Serve immediately.
Per Serving: Calories 154; Fat 10.98g; Sodium 225mg; Carbs 4.69g; Fiber 1.7g; Sugar 1.75g; Protein 9.99g

Easy Baked "Hard-Boiled" Eggs

⏱ Prep: 2 minutes 🍲 Cook: 18 minutes ❧ Serves: 4

Ingredients:

4 large eggs
1 cup water

Preparation:

1. Place eggs into a 4-cup round baking-safe dish and pour water over eggs. 2. Insert the wire rack into the bottom rack height position. Close the oven door. Turn the FUNCTION dial until the indicator on the LCD screen reaches the BAKE function. Set the temperature to 300°F and set the timer to 18 minutes. Press START/CANCEL to activate. 3. When preheating has completed, place the round dish on the wire rack and bake for 18 minutes. 4. Store cooked eggs in the refrigerator until ready to use or peel and eat warm.
Per Serving: Calories 72; Fat 4.76g; Sodium 72mg; Carbs 0.36g; Fiber 0g; Sugar 0.19g; Protein 6.28g

Cheesy Scrambled Eggs

⏰ Prep: 5 minutes 🍲 Cook: 15 minutes 🍃 Serves: 2

Ingredients:

4 large eggs
2 tablespoons unsalted butter, melted
½ cup shredded sharp Cheddar cheese

Preparation:

1. Crack eggs into 2-cup round baking dish and whisk. 2. Insert the wire rack into the bottom rack height position. Close the oven door. Turn the FUNCTION dial until the indicator on the LCD screen reaches the BAKE function. Set the temperature to 400°F and set the timer to 10 minutes. Press START/CANCEL to activate. 3. When preheating has completed, place the round dish on the wire rack and bake. 4. After 5 minutes, stir the eggs and add the butter and cheese. Let cook 3 more minutes and stir again. 5. Allow eggs to finish cooking an additional 2 minutes or remove if they are to your desired liking. 6. Use a fork to fluff. Serve warm.
Per Serving: Calories 328; Fat 26.78g; Sodium 329mg; Carbs 1.1g; Fiber 0g; Sugar 0.45g; Protein 19.81g

Cinnamon Cheese Bread Sticks

⏰ Prep: 10 minutes 🍲 Cook: 7 minutes 🍃 Serves: 4

Ingredients:

1 cup shredded mozzarella cheese
1 ounce full-fat cream cheese
⅓ cup blanched finely ground almond flour
½ teaspoon baking soda
½ cup granular erythritol, divided
1 teaspoon vanilla extract
1 large egg
2 tablespoons unsalted butter, melted
½ teaspoon ground cinnamon
3 tablespoons powdered erythritol
2 teaspoons unsweetened vanilla almond milk

Preparation:

1. Place mozzarella in a large microwave-safe bowl and break cream cheese into small pieces and place into bowl. Microwave for 45 seconds. 2. Stir in almond flour, baking soda, ¼ cup granular erythritol, and vanilla. A soft dough should form. Microwave the mix for additional 15 seconds if it becomes too stiff. 3. Mix egg into the dough, using your hands if necessary. 4. Cut a piece of parchment to fit the baking pan. Press the dough into an 8" × 5" rectangle on the parchment and cut into eight (1") sticks. 5. In a small bowl, mix butter, cinnamon, and remaining granular erythritol. Brush half the mixture over the top of the sticks. 6. Insert the wire rack into the bottom rack height position. Close the oven door. Turn the FUNCTION dial until the indicator on the LCD screen reaches the BAKE function. Set the temperature to 400°F and set the timer to 7 minutes. Press START/CANCEL to activate. 7. When preheating has completed, place the baking pan on the wire rack and bake for 7 minutes. 8. Halfway through the cooking time, flip the sticks and brush with remaining butter mixture. When done, sticks should be crispy. 9. To make glaze, whisk powdered erythritol and almond milk in a small bowl. Drizzle over cinnamon sticks. Serve warm.
Per Serving: Calories 262; Fat 12.39g; Sodium 423mg; Carbs 26.45g; Fiber 1.9g; Sugar 21.85g; Protein 13.17g

Sausage Egg & Cheese Breakfast Calzone

⏲ **Prep:** 15 minutes   🍲 **Cook:** 15 minutes   ≋ **Serves:** 4

Ingredients:

1½ cups shredded mozzarella cheese
½ cup blanched finely ground almond flour
1 ounce full-fat cream cheese
1 large whole egg
4 large eggs, scrambled
½ pound cooked breakfast sausage, crumbled
8 tablespoons shredded mild Cheddar cheese

Preparation:

1. In a large microwave-safe bowl, add mozzarella, almond flour, and cream cheese. Microwave for 1 minute. Stir until the mixture is smooth and forms a ball. Add the egg and stir until dough forms. 2. Place dough between two sheets of parchment and roll out to ¼" thickness. Cut the dough into four rectangles. 3. Mix scrambled eggs and cooked sausage together in a large bowl. Divide the mixture evenly among each piece of dough, placing it on the lower half of the rectangle. Sprinkle each with 2 tablespoons Cheddar. 4. Fold over the rectangle to cover the egg and meat mixture. Pinch, roll, or use a wet fork to close the edges completely. 5. Cut a piece of parchment to fit the baking pan and place the calzones inside. 6. Insert the wire rack into the middle rack height position. Close the oven door. Turn the FUNCTION dial until the indicator on the LCD screen reaches the BAKE function. Set the temperature to 380°F and set the timer to 15 minutes. Press START/CANCEL to activate. 7. When preheating has completed, place the baking pan on the wire rack and bake for 7 minutes. 8. Flip the calzones halfway through the cooking time. When done, calzones should be golden in color. Serve immediately.
Per Serving: Calories 385; Fat 21.99g; Sodium 1318mg; Carbs 9.84g; Fiber 1.9g; Sugar 4.06g; Protein 36.38g

Cheese Sausage Balls

⏲ **Prep:** 10 minutes   🍲 **Cook:** 12 minutes   ≋ **Serves:** 4

Ingredients:

1-pound pork breakfast sausage
½ cup shredded Cheddar cheese
1 ounce full-fat cream cheese, softened
1 large egg

Preparation:

1. Mix all ingredients in a large bowl. Form into sixteen (1") balls. Place the balls into the baking pan. 2. Insert the wire rack into the bottom rack height position. Close the oven door. Turn the FUNCTION dial until the indicator on the LCD screen reaches the BAKE function. Set the temperature to 400°F and set the timer to 12 minutes. Press START/CANCEL to activate. 3. When preheating has completed, place the baking pan on the wire rack and bake for 12 minutes. 4. Flip them two or three times during cooking. Sausage balls will be browned on the outside and have an internal temperature of at least 145°F when completely cooked. 5. Serve warm.
Per Serving: Calories 482; Fat 42.58g; Sodium 963mg; Carbs 1.59g; Fiber 0g; Sugar 0.5g; Protein 21.68g

Breakfast Spaghetti Squash Fritters

⏱ **Prep: 15 minutes**   🍲 **Cook: 8 minutes**   ❦ **Serves: 4**

Ingredients:

2 cups cooked spaghetti squash
2 tablespoons unsalted butter, softened
1 large egg
¼ cup blanched finely ground almond flour
2 stalks green onion, sliced
½ teaspoon garlic powder
1 teaspoon dried parsley

Preparation:

1. Remove excess moisture from the squash using a cheesecloth or kitchen towel. 2. Mix all ingredients in a large bowl. Form into four patties. 3. Cut a piece of parchment to fit the baking pan. Place each patty on the parchment inside the pan. 4. Insert the wire rack into the middle rack height position. Close the oven door. Turn the FUNCTION dial until the indicator on the LCD screen reaches the BAKE function. Set the temperature to 400°F and set the timer to 8 minutes. Press START/CANCEL to activate. 5. When preheating has completed, place the baking pan on the wire rack and bake for 8 minutes. 6. Flip the patties halfway through the cooking time. Serve warm.
Per Serving: Calories 89; Fat 5.3g; Sodium 42mg; Carbs 7.05g; Fiber 1.8g; Sugar 2.56g; Protein 4.4g

Ham Egg Cups

⏱ **Prep: 5 minutes**   🍲 **Cook: 15 minutes**   ❦ **Serves: 2**

Ingredients:

4 slices deli ham
¼ cup shredded Cheddar cheese
4 large eggs
1 tablespoon chopped fresh parsley (optional)
Salt and freshly ground black pepper

Preparation:

1. Lightly coat 4 silicone muffin cups with vegetable oil. 2. Line each cup with a piece of ham, tearing it into a few smaller pieces, if necessary, to ensure an even fit. (It's OK if the ham extends slightly above the top of the cup.) Sprinkle 1 tablespoon of cheese into the bottom of each cup, then crack an egg into each. 3. Insert the wire rack into the bottom rack height position. Close the oven door. Turn the FUNCTION dial until the indicator on the LCD screen reaches the BAKE function. Set the temperature to 400°F and set the timer to 15 minutes. Press START/CANCEL to activate. 4. When preheating has completed, place the muffin cups on the wire rack and bake for 15 minutes. Bake until the whites are set and the yolk is cooked to the desired doneness. 5. Scatter parsley on top, if desired, and season to taste with salt and pepper.
Per Serving: Calories 248; Fat 15.87g; Sodium 1055mg; Carbs 1.47g; Fiber 0.1g; Sugar 0.43g; Protein 23.79g

Breakfast Egg Pizza

⏱ Prep: 10 minutes　　🍳 Cook: 24 minutes　　🍲 Serves: 2

Ingredients:

4 large eggs, divided
1 tablespoon water
½ teaspoon garlic powder
½ teaspoon onion powder
½ teaspoon dried oregano
2 tablespoons coconut flour
3 tablespoons grated Parmesan cheese
½ cup shredded provolone cheese
1 link cooked turkey sausage, chopped (about 2 ounces)
2 sun-dried tomatoes, finely chopped
2 scallions, thinly sliced

Preparation:

1. Line an 8-inch cake pan with parchment paper and lightly coat the paper with olive oil. 2. In a large bowl, whisk 2 of the eggs with the water, garlic powder, onion powder, and dried oregano. Add the coconut flour, breaking up any lumps with your hands as you add it to the bowl. Add the coconut flour to the egg mixture, mixing until smooth. Stir in the Parmesan cheese. Allow the mixture to rest for a few minutes until thick and dough-like. 3. Transfer the mixture to the prepared pan. Use a spatula to spread it evenly and slightly up the sides of the pan. 4. Insert the wire rack into the middle rack height position. Close the oven door. Turn the FUNCTION dial until the indicator on the LCD screen reaches the BAKE function. Set the temperature to 400°F and set the timer to 10 minutes. Press START/CANCEL to activate. 5. When preheating has completed, place the cake pan on the wire rack and bake for 10 minutes. Bake until the crust is set but still light in color. Top with the cheeses, sausage, and sun-dried tomatoes. 6. Break the remaining 2 eggs into a small bowl, then slide them onto the pizza. Return the pizza to the oven. Bake for 10 to 14 minutes until the egg whites are set and the yolks are the desired doneness. 7. Top with the scallions and allow to rest for 5 minutes before serving.
Per Serving: Calories 396; Fat 23.7g; Sodium 788mg; Carbs 15.98g; Fiber 2.1g; Sugar 3.06g; Protein 30.12g

Breakfast Blueberry Muffins

⏱ Prep: 10 minutes　　🍳 Cook: 25 minutes　　🍲 Serves: 6

Ingredients:

1¼ cups almond flour
3 tablespoons Swerve sugar replacement
1 teaspoon baking powder
2 large eggs
3 tablespoons melted butter
1 tablespoon milk
1 tablespoon fresh lemon juice
½ cup fresh blueberries

Preparation:

1. Lightly coat 6 silicone muffin cups with vegetable oil. Set aside. 2. In a large mixing bowl, combine the almond flour, Swerve, and baking soda. Set aside. 3. In a separate small bowl, whisk together the eggs, butter, milk, and lemon juice. Add the egg mixture to the flour mixture and stir until just combined. Fold in the blueberries and let the batter sit for 5 minutes. 4. Spoon the muffin batter into the muffin cups, about two-thirds full. 5. Insert the wire rack into the middle rack height position. Close the oven door. Turn the FUNCTION dial until the indicator on the LCD screen reaches the BAKE function. Set the temperature to 350°F and set the timer to 25 minutes. Press START/CANCEL to activate. 6. When preheating has completed, place the muffin cups on the wire rack and bake for 25 minutes. Bake until a toothpick inserted into the center of a muffin comes out clean. 7. Remove them from the oven and let the muffins cool for about 5 minutes before transferring them to a wire rack to cool completely.
Per Serving: Calories 185; Fat 8.1g; Sodium 27mg; Carbs 24.58g; Fiber 3g; Sugar 5.5g; Protein 5.64g

Homemade Biscuits

🕑 Prep: 15 minutes   🍲 Cook: 15 minutes   🍃 Serves: 12

Ingredients:

10 ounces (2¼ cups plus 2 tablespoons) finely ground blanched almond flour
1½ tablespoons baking powder
1 teaspoon garlic powder
1 teaspoon sea salt
½ teaspoon freshly ground black pepper
¼ teaspoon xanthan gum
3 tablespoons unsalted butter, melted, divided
1 large egg, beaten
¾ cup heavy (whipping) cream
¾ cup shredded Cheddar cheese (optional)

Preparation:

1. In a large bowl, whisk together the almond flour, baking powder, garlic powder, salt, pepper, and xanthan gum. 2. In a small bowl, whisk together 1 tablespoon of the melted butter, the egg, and the heavy cream. 3. Add the wet mixture to the dry mixture and stir, just until the dough comes together. Stir in the Cheddar cheese (if using). 4. Place the dough on a sheet of parchment paper and press it out evenly to a ½-inch thickness. 5. Using a 2½-inch round cookie cutter, cut the dough into biscuits. Ball up the dough scraps, press it out again, and continue cutting biscuits until all the dough is used. 6. Working in batches, place the biscuits in either silicone muffin cups or in a 7-inch cake pan that fits in your oven. Brush the tops and sides of the biscuits with the remaining 2 tablespoons of butter. 7. Insert the wire rack into the middle rack height position. Close the oven door. Turn the FUNCTION dial until the indicator on the LCD screen reaches the BAKE function. Set the temperature to 325°F and set the timer to 12 minutes. Press START/CANCEL to activate. 8. When preheating has completed, place the muffin cups on the wire rack and bake for 12 minutes. Then check for doneness. Cook for up to 3 minutes more, until golden brown.

Per Serving: Calories 133; Fat 5.7g; Sodium 206mg; Carbs 18.5g; Fiber 2.7g; Sugar 0.33g; Protein 3.98g

Broccoli Frittata

🕑 Prep: 7 minutes   🍲 Cook: 23 minutes   🍃 Serves: 2

Ingredients:

Avocado oil spray
¼ cup diced red onion
¼ cup diced red bell pepper
¼ cup finely chopped broccoli
4 large eggs
3 ounces shredded sharp Cheddar cheese, divided
½ teaspoon dried thyme
Sea salt
Freshly ground black pepper

Preparation:

1. Spray a 7-inch pan well with oil. Put the onion, pepper, and broccoli in the pan. 2. Insert the wire rack into the middle rack height position. Close the oven door. Turn the FUNCTION dial until the indicator on the LCD screen reaches the BAKE function. Set the temperature to 350°F and set the timer to 5 minutes. Press START/CANCEL to activate. 3. When preheating has completed, place the pan on the wire rack and bake for 5 minutes. 4. While the vegetables cook, beat the eggs in a medium bowl. Stir in half of the cheese, and season with the thyme, salt, and pepper. 5. Add the eggs to the pan and top with the remaining cheese. Bake at 350°F for 16 to 18 minutes, until cooked through.

Per Serving: Calories 249; Fat 15.62g; Sodium 846mg; Carbs 7.67g; Fiber 0.7g; Sugar 4.49g; Protein 18.73g

Crustless Cheese Spinach Frittata

⏱ **Prep: 10 minutes**   🍲 **Cook: 20 minutes**   ❧ **Serves: 4**

❱ Ingredients:

6 large eggs
½ cup heavy whipping cream
1 cup frozen chopped spinach, drained
1 cup shredded sharp Cheddar cheese
¼ cup peeled and diced yellow onion
½ teaspoon salt
¼ teaspoon ground black pepper

❱ Preparation:

1. In a large bowl, whisk eggs and cream together. Whisk in spinach, Cheddar, onion, salt, and pepper. 2. Pour mixture into an ungreased 6" round nonstick baking dish. Insert the wire rack into the middle rack height position. Close the oven door. Turn the FUNCTION dial until the indicator on the LCD screen reaches the BAKE function. Set the temperature to 320°F and set the timer to 20 minutes. Press START/CANCEL to activate. 3. When preheating has completed, place the baking dish on the wire rack and bake for 20 minutes. 4. Eggs will be firm and slightly browned when done. Serve immediately.

Per Serving: Calories 293; Fat 23.05g; Sodium 614mg; Carbs 3.5g; Fiber 1.3g; Sugar 1.27g; Protein 18g

Spinach-Bacon Egg Muffins

⏱ **Prep: 10 minutes**   🍲 **Cook: 14 minutes**   ❧ **Serves: 6**

❱ Ingredients:

6 large eggs
¼ cup heavy (whipping) cream
½ teaspoon sea salt
¼ teaspoon freshly ground black pepper
¼ teaspoon cayenne pepper (optional)
¾ cup frozen chopped spinach, thawed and drained
4 strips cooked bacon, crumbled
2 ounces shredded Cheddar cheese

❱ Preparation:

1. In a large bowl (with a spout if you have one), whisk together the eggs, heavy cream, salt, black pepper, and cayenne pepper (if using). 2. Divide the spinach and bacon among 6 silicone muffin cups. Divide the egg mixture among the muffin cups. Top with the cheese. 3. Insert the wire rack into the bottom rack height position. Close the oven door. Turn the FUNCTION dial until the indicator on the LCD screen reaches the BAKE function. Set the temperature to 300°F and set the timer to 14 minutes. Press START/CANCEL to activate. 4. When preheating has completed, place the pan on the wire rack and bake for 14 minutes. Bake until the eggs are set and cooked through.

Per Serving: Calories 144; Fat 10.91g; Sodium 391mg; Carbs 1.77g; Fiber 0.7g; Sugar 0.49g; Protein 9.74g

Smoky Pork Patties

⏱ **Prep: 10 minutes**   🍲 **Cook: 9 minutes**   ❧ **Serves: 8**

❭ **Ingredients:**

1-pound ground pork
1 tablespoon coconut aminos
2 teaspoons liquid smoke
1 teaspoon dried sage
1 teaspoon sea salt
½ teaspoon fennel seeds
½ teaspoon dried thyme
½ teaspoon freshly ground black pepper
¼ teaspoon cayenne pepper

❭ **Preparation:**

1. In a large bowl, combine the pork, coconut aminos, liquid smoke, sage, salt, fennel seeds, thyme, black pepper, and cayenne pepper. Work the meat with your hands until the seasonings are fully incorporated. 2. Shape the mixture into 8 equal-sized patties. Using your thumb, make a dent in the center of each patty. Place the patties on a plate and cover with plastic wrap. Refrigerate the patties for at least 30 minutes. 3. Working in batches if necessary, place the patties in a single layer on the broiling rack inserted into the baking pan, being careful not to overcrowd them. 4. Insert the wire rack into the bottom rack height position. Close the oven door. Turn the FUNCTION dial until the indicator on the LCD screen reaches the ROAST function. Set the temperature to 400°F and set the timer to 5 minutes. Press START/CANCEL to activate. 5. When preheating has completed, place the baking pan on the wire rack and cook for 5 minutes. Flip and cook for about 4 minutes more. Serve warm.
Per Serving: Calories 170; Fat 11.83g; Sodium 334mg; Carbs 0.34g; Fiber 0.2g; Sugar 0.06g; Protein 14.63g

Classic Pancake

⏱ **Prep: 5 minutes**   🍲 **Cook: 30 minutes**   ❧ **Serves: 2**

❭ **Ingredients:**

1 cup blanched finely ground almond flour
2 tablespoons granular erythritol
1 tablespoon salted butter, melted
1 large egg
⅓ cup unsweetened almond milk
½ teaspoon vanilla extract

❭ **Preparation:**

1. In a large bowl, mix all ingredients together, then pour half the batter into an ungreased 6" round nonstick baking dish. 2. Insert the wire rack into the middle rack height position. Close the oven door. Turn the FUNCTION dial until the indicator on the LCD screen reaches the BAKE function. Set the temperature to 320°F and set the timer to 15 minutes. Press START/CANCEL to activate. 3. When preheating has completed, place the baking dish on the wire rack and bake for 15 minutes. 4. The pancake will be golden brown on top and firm, and a toothpick inserted in the center will come out clean when done. Repeat with remaining batter. 5. Slice in half in dish and serve warm.
Per Serving: Calories 237; Fat 6.85g; Sodium 149mg; Carbs 26.42g; Fiber 4.9g; Sugar 18.11g; Protein 19.09g

Mushroom Quesadilla

⏰ **Prep: 10 minutes**   🍲 **Cook: 5 minutes**   🗇 **Serves: 2**

▶ Ingredients:

1 tablespoon coconut oil
½ medium green bell pepper, seeded and chopped
¼ cup diced red onion
¼ cup chopped white mushrooms
4 flatbread dough tortillas
⅔ cup shredded pepper jack cheese
½ medium avocado, peeled, pitted, and mashed
¼ cup full-fat sour cream
¼ cup mild salsa

▶ Preparation:

1. In a medium skillet over medium heat, warm coconut oil. Add pepper, onion, and mushrooms to skillet and sauté until peppers begin to soften, 3–5 minutes. 2. Place two tortillas on a work surface and sprinkle each with half of cheese. Top with sautéed veggies, sprinkle with remaining cheese, and place remaining two tortillas on top. Place quesadillas carefully on the broiling rack inserted into the baking pan. 3. Insert the wire rack into the bottom rack height position. Close the oven door. Turn the FUNCTION dial until the indicator on the LCD screen reaches the ROAST function. Set the temperature to 400°F and set the timer to 5 minutes. Press START/CANCEL to activate. 4. When preheating has completed, place the baking pan on the wire rack and cook for 5 minutes. 5. Flip the quesadillas halfway through the cooking time. Serve warm with avocado, sour cream, and salsa.
Per Serving: Calories 601; Fat 31.31g; Sodium 1169mg; Carbs 62.44g; Fiber 7.2g; Sugar 6.62g; Protein 19.9g

Spinach, Artichoke & Cauliflower Casserole

⏰ **Prep: 15 minutes**   🍲 **Cook: 15 minutes**   🗇 **Serves: 4**

▶ Ingredients:

1 tablespoon salted butter, melted
¼ cup diced yellow onion
8 ounces full-fat cream cheese, softened
⅓ cup full-fat mayonnaise
⅓ cup full-fat sour cream
¼ cup chopped pickled jalapeños
2 cups fresh spinach, chopped
2 cups cauliflower florets, chopped
1 cup artichoke hearts, chopped

▶ Preparation:

1. In a large bowl, mix butter, onion, cream cheese, mayonnaise, and sour cream. Fold in jalapeños, spinach, cauliflower, and artichokes. 2. Pour the mixture into a 4-cup round baking dish and cover with foil. 3. Insert the wire rack into the bottom rack height position. Close the oven door. Turn the FUNCTION dial until the indicator on the LCD screen reaches the BAKE function. Set the temperature to 370°F and set the timer to 15 minutes. Press START/CANCEL to activate. 4. When preheating has completed, place the baking dish on the wire rack and bake for 15 minutes. 5. In the last 2 minutes of cooking, remove the foil to brown the top. Serve warm.
Per Serving: Calories 237; Fat 15.01g; Sodium 341mg; Carbs 19.74g; Fiber 4.3g; Sugar 6.2g; Protein 8.3g

Classic Eggplant Lasagna

⏱ **Prep: 10 minutes**　🍴 **Cook: 46 minutes**　🍲 **Serves: 4**

Ingredients:

1 small eggplant (about ¾ pound), sliced into rounds
2 teaspoons salt
1 tablespoon olive oil
1 cup shredded mozzarella, divided
1 cup ricotta cheese
1 large egg
¼ cup grated Parmesan cheese
½ teaspoon dried oregano
1½ cups no-sugar-added marinara
1 tablespoon chopped fresh parsley

Preparation:

1. Coat a 6-cup casserole dish that fits in your oven with olive oil; set aside. 2. Arrange the eggplant slices in a single layer on a baking sheet and sprinkle with the salt. Let sit for 10 minutes. Use a paper towel to remove the excess moisture and salt. 3. Working in batches if necessary, brush the eggplant with the olive oil and arrange in a single layer in the baking pan. 4. Insert the wire rack into the bottom rack height position. Close the oven door. Turn the FUNCTION dial until the indicator on the LCD screen reaches the BAKE function. Set the temperature to 350°F and set the timer to 6 minutes. Press START/CANCEL to activate. 5. When preheating has completed, place the baking pan on the wire rack and bake for 6 minutes. Flip the eggplant halfway through the cooking time. 6. Transfer the eggplant back to the baking sheet and let cool. 7. In a small bowl, combine ½ cup of the mozzarella with the ricotta, egg, Parmesan, and oregano. 8. To assemble the lasagna, spread a spoonful of marinara in the bottom of the casserole dish, followed by a layer of eggplant, a layer of the cheese mixture, and a layer of marinara. Repeat the layers until all of the ingredients are used, ending with the remaining ½ cup of mozzarella. Scatter the parsley on top. Cover the baking dish with foil. 9. Increase the oven temperature to 370°F and bake for 30 minutes. Uncover the dish and continue baking for 10 minutes longer until the cheese begins to brown. Let the casserole sit for at least 10 minutes before serving.
Per Serving: Calories 306; Fat 16.04g; Sodium 1588mg; Carbs 19.8g; Fiber 6.4g; Sugar 10.79g; Protein 22.02g

Cheese Zucchini Tart

⏱ **Prep: 15 minutes**　🍴 **Cook: 1 hour**　🍲 **Serves: 6**

Ingredients:

½ cup grated Parmesan cheese, divided
1½ cups almond flour
1 tablespoon coconut flour
½ teaspoon garlic powder
¾ teaspoon salt, divided
¼ cup unsalted butter, melted
1 zucchini, thinly sliced (about 2 cups)
1 cup ricotta cheese
3 eggs
2 tablespoons heavy cream
2 cloves garlic, minced
½ teaspoon dried tarragon

Preparation:

1. Coat a round 6-cup pan with olive oil and set aside. 2. In a large bowl, whisk ¼ cup of the Parmesan with the almond flour, coconut flour, garlic powder, and ¼ teaspoon of the salt. Stir in the melted butter until the dough resembles coarse crumbs. Press the dough firmly into the bottom and up the sides of the prepared pan. 3. Insert the wire rack into the middle rack height position. Close the oven door. Turn the FUNCTION dial until the indicator on the LCD screen reaches the BAKE function. Set the temperature to 330°F and set the timer to 15 minutes. Press START/CANCEL to activate. 4. When preheating has completed, place the baking pan on the wire rack and bake for 15 minutes. Bake until the crust begins to brown. Let cool to room temperature. 5. Meanwhile, place the zucchini in a colander and sprinkle with the remaining ½ teaspoon salt. Toss gently to distribute the salt and let sit for 30 minutes. Pat the zucchini dry with paper towels. 6. In a large bowl, whisk together the ricotta, eggs, heavy cream, garlic, and tarragon. Gently stir in the zucchini slices. Pour the cheese mixture into the cooled crust and sprinkle with the remaining ¼ cup Parmesan. 7. Increase the oven temperature to 350°F. Place the pan in the oven and bake for 45 to 50 minutes, or until set and a tester inserted into the center of the tart comes out clean. Serve warm or at room temperature.
Per Serving: Calories 255; Fat 16.88g; Sodium 542mg; Carbs 8.62g; Fiber 2.5g; Sugar 1.65g; Protein 18.21g

Crispy Broccoli-Cheese Fritters

⏱ Prep: 10 minutes   🍲 Cook: 25 minutes   🍃 Serves: 4

▶ Ingredients:

1 cup broccoli florets
1 cup shredded mozzarella cheese
¾ cup almond flour
½ cup flaxseed meal, divided
2 teaspoons baking powder
1 teaspoon garlic powder
Salt and freshly ground black pepper
2 eggs, lightly beaten
½ cup ranch dressing

▶ Preparation:

1. In a food processor fitted with a metal blade, pulse the broccoli until very finely chopped. 2. Transfer the broccoli to a large bowl and add the mozzarella, almond flour, ¼ cup of the flaxseed meal, baking powder, and garlic powder. Stir until thoroughly combined. Season to taste with salt and black pepper. Add the eggs and stir again to form a sticky dough. Shape the dough into 1¼-inch fritters. 3. Place the remaining ¼ cup flaxseed meal in a shallow bowl and roll the fritters in the meal to form an even coating. 4. Working in batches if necessary, arrange the fritters in a single layer in the baking pan and spray generously with olive oil. 5. Insert the wire rack into the bottom rack height position. Close the oven door. Turn the FUNCTION dial until the indicator on the LCD screen reaches the BAKE function. Set the temperature to 400°F and set the timer to 25 minutes. Press START/CANCEL to activate. 6. When preheating has completed, place the baking pan on the wire rack and bake for 25 minutes. Flip them halfway through the cooking time. Bake until the fritters are golden brown and crispy. 7. Serve with the ranch dressing for dipping.

Per Serving: Calories 354; Fat 24.43g; Sodium 777mg; Carbs 14.86g; Fiber 8.4g; Sugar 3.21g; Protein 22.28g

Crispy Tofu with Sesame Seeds

⏱ Prep: 10 minutes   🍲 Cook: 20 minutes   🍃 Serves: 4

▶ Ingredients:

1 (16-ounce) block extra-firm tofu
2 tablespoons reduced-sodium soy sauce
1 tablespoon toasted sesame oil
1 tablespoon olive oil
1 tablespoon chili-garlic sauce
1½ teaspoons sesame seeds
1 scallion, thinly sliced

▶ Preparation:

1. Press the tofu for at least 15 minutes by wrapping it in paper towels and setting a heavy pan on top so that the moisture drains. 2. Slice the tofu into bite-size cubes and transfer to a bowl. Drizzle with the soy sauce, sesame oil, olive oil, and chili-garlic sauce. Cover and refrigerate for 1 hour or up to overnight. 3. Arrange the tofu in a single layer in the baking pan. Insert the wire rack into the bottom rack height position. Close the oven door. Turn the FUNCTION dial until the indicator on the LCD screen reaches the BAKE function. Set the temperature to 400°F and set the timer to 20 minutes. Press START/CANCEL to activate. 4. When preheating has completed, place the baking pan on the wire rack and bake for 20 minutes. Pausing to shake the pan halfway through the cooking time. 5. Serve with any juices that accumulate in the bottom of the pan, sprinkled with the sesame seeds and sliced scallion.

Per Serving: Calories 198; Fat 15.49g; Sodium 188mg; Carbs 5.33g; Fiber 1g; Sugar 2.6g; Protein 12.16g

Spicy Roasted Bok Choy with Sesame Seeds

⏱ Prep: 10 minutes 🍲 Cook: 10 minutes 🥬 Serves: 4

Ingredients:

2 tablespoons olive oil
2 tablespoons reduced-sodium soy sauce
2 teaspoons sesame oil
2 teaspoons chili-garlic sauce
2 cloves garlic, minced
1 head (about 1 pound) bok choy, sliced lengthwise into quarters
2 teaspoons sesame seeds

Preparation:

1. In a large bowl, combine the olive oil, soy sauce, sesame oil, chili-garlic sauce, and garlic. Add the bok choy and toss, massaging the leaves with your hands if necessary, until thoroughly coated. 2. Arrange the bok choy in the baking pan. Insert the wire rack into the bottom rack height position. Close the oven door. Turn the FUNCTION dial until the indicator on the LCD screen reaches the BAKE function. Set the temperature to 400°F and set the timer to 10 minutes. Press START/CANCEL to activate. 3. When preheating has completed, place the baking pan on the wire rack and bake for 10 minutes. Pausing about halfway through the cooking time to flip the food. Cook until the bok choy is tender and the tips of the leaves begin to crisp. 4. Remove from the oven and allow to cool for a few minutes before coarsely chopping. Serve sprinkled with the sesame seeds.

Per Serving: Calories 131; Fat 11.51g; Sodium 233mg; Carbs 5.67g; Fiber 1.7g; Sugar 3.2g; Protein 2.71g

Roasted Brussels Sprouts with Pecans

⏱ Prep: 10 minutes 🍲 Cook: 27 minutes 🥬 Serves: 4

Ingredients:

½ cup pecans
1½ pounds fresh Brussels sprouts, trimmed and quartered
2 tablespoons olive oil
Salt and freshly ground black pepper
¼ cup crumbled Gorgonzola cheese

Preparation:

1. Spread the pecans in a single layer in the baking pan. 2. Insert the wire rack into the bottom rack height position. Close the oven door. Turn the FUNCTION dial until the indicator on the LCD screen reaches the ROAST function. Set the temperature to 350°F and set the timer to 5 minutes. Press START/CANCEL to activate. 3. When preheating has completed, place the baking pan on the wire rack and cook for 5 minutes. Roast until the pecans are lightly browned and fragrant. Transfer the pecans to a plate and continue preheating the oven, increasing the heat to 400°F. 4. In a large bowl, toss the Brussels sprouts with the olive oil and season with salt and black pepper to taste. 5. Working in batches if necessary, arrange the Brussels sprouts in a single layer in the baking pan. Roast in the preheated oven for 22 minutes, or until the sprouts are tender and starting to brown on the edges. Flip them halfway through the cooking time. 6. Transfer the sprouts to a serving bowl and top with the toasted pecans and Gorgonzola. Serve warm or at room temperature.

Per Serving: Calories 248; Fat 18.6g; Sodium 333mg; Carbs 17.14g; Fiber 7.7g; Sugar 4.28g; Protein 8.69g

Savory Buttered Mushrooms

⏱ **Prep: 10 minutes**   🍽 **Cook: 10 minutes**   ❧ **Serves: 4**

❱ Ingredients:

8 ounces cremini mushrooms
2 tablespoons salted butter, melted
¼ teaspoon salt
¼ teaspoon ground black pepper

❱ Preparation:

1. In a medium bowl, toss mushrooms with butter, then sprinkle with salt and pepper. Place on the broiling rack inserted into the baking pan. 2. Insert the wire rack into the bottom rack height position. Close the oven door. Turn the FUNCTION dial until the indicator on the LCD screen reaches the ROAST function. Set the temperature to 400°F and set the timer to 10 minutes. Press START/CANCEL to activate. 3. When preheating has completed, place the baking pan on the wire rack and cook for 10 minutes. Carefully shake the pan halfway through cooking. Mushrooms will be tender when done. 4. Serve warm.
Per Serving: Calories 202; Fat 4.38g; Sodium 184mg; Carbs 42.83g; Fiber 6.6g; Sugar 1.26g; Protein 5.49g

Cheese Zucchini Fritters

⏱ **Prep: 10 minutes**   🍽 **Cook: 10 minutes**   ❧ **Serves: 4**

❱ Ingredients:

2 zucchinis, grated (about 1 pound)
1 teaspoon salt
¼ cup almond flour
¼ cup grated Parmesan cheese
1 large egg
¼ teaspoon dried thyme
¼ teaspoon ground turmeric
¼ teaspoon freshly ground black pepper
1 tablespoon olive oil
½ lemon, sliced into wedges

❱ Preparation:

1. Cut a piece of parchment paper to fit slightly smaller than the baking pan. 2. Place the zucchini in a large colander and sprinkle with the salt. Let sit for 5 to 10 minutes. Squeeze as much liquid as you can from the zucchini and place in a large mixing bowl. Add the almond flour, Parmesan, egg, thyme, turmeric, and black pepper. Stir gently until thoroughly combined. 3. Shape the mixture into 8 patties and arrange on the parchment paper. Brush lightly with the olive oil. 4. Insert the wire rack into the bottom rack height position. Close the oven door. Turn the FUNCTION dial until the indicator on the LCD screen reaches the BAKE function. Set the temperature to 400°F and set the timer to 10 minutes. Press START/CANCEL to activate. 5. When preheating has completed, place the baking pan on the wire rack and bake for 10 minutes until golden brown. Pausing halfway through the cooking time to turn the patties. 6. Serve warm with the lemon wedges.
Per Serving: Calories 103; Fat 6.54g; Sodium 712mg; Carbs 7.18g; Fiber 1g; Sugar 0.24g; Protein 4.54g

Roasted Buttered Asparagus

⏱ **Prep: 5 minutes**　🍲 **Cook: 12 minutes**　✦ **Serves: 4**

Ingredients:

1 tablespoon olive oil
1-pound asparagus spears, ends trimmed
¼ teaspoon salt
¼ teaspoon ground black pepper
1 tablespoon salted butter, melted

Preparation:

1. In a large bowl, drizzle olive oil over asparagus spears and sprinkle with salt and pepper. 2. Place spears on the broiling rack inserted into the baking pan. Insert the wire rack into the bottom rack height position. 3. Close the oven door. Turn the FUNCTION dial until the indicator on the LCD screen reaches the ROAST function. Set the temperature to 375°F and set the timer to 12 minutes. Press START/CANCEL to activate. 4. When preheating has completed, place the baking pan on the wire rack and cook for 12 minutes. 5. Carefully shake the pan halfway through cooking. Asparagus will be lightly browned and tender when done. 6. Transfer to a large dish and drizzle with butter. Serve warm.
Per Serving: Calories 70; Fat 5.42g; Sodium 163mg; Carbs 4.5g; Fiber 2.4g; Sugar 2.13g; Protein 2.53g

Simple Caramelized Broccoli

⏱ **Prep: 5 minutes**　🍲 **Cook: 8 minutes**　✦ **Serves: 4**

Ingredients:

4 cups broccoli florets
3 tablespoons melted ghee or butter-flavored coconut oil
1½ teaspoons fine sea salt or smoked salt
Mayonnaise, for serving (optional; omit for egg-free)

Preparation:

1. Spray the baking pan with avocado oil. 2. Place the broccoli in a large bowl. Drizzle it with the ghee, toss to coat, and sprinkle it with the salt. Transfer the broccoli to the baking pan. 3. Insert the wire rack into the bottom rack height position. Close the oven door. Turn the FUNCTION dial until the indicator on the LCD screen reaches the BAKE function. Set the temperature to 400°F and set the timer to 8 minutes. Press START/CANCEL to activate. 4. When preheating has completed, place the baking pan on the wire rack and bake for 8 minutes. 5. Store leftovers in an airtight container in the fridge for up to 4 days or in the freezer for up to a month.
Per Serving: Calories 97; Fat 10.4g; Sodium 885mg; Carbs 1.14g; Fiber 1.1g; Sugar 0.15g; Protein 1.27g

Provencal Tomatoes

⏱ **Prep: 10 minutes**   🍲 **Cook: 15 minutes**   🍃 **Serves: 4**

Ingredients:

4 small ripe tomatoes connected on the vine
¼ teaspoon fine sea salt
¼ teaspoon ground black pepper
½ cup powdered Parmesan cheese (about 1½ ounces)
2 tablespoons chopped fresh parsley
¼ cup minced onions
2 cloves garlic, minced
½ teaspoon chopped fresh thyme leaves
For Garnish:
Fresh parsley leaves
Ground black pepper
Sprig of fresh basil

Preparation:

1. Spray the baking pan with avocado oil. 2. Slice the tops off the tomatoes without removing them from the vine. Do not discard the tops. Use a large spoon to scoop the seeds out of the tomatoes. Sprinkle the insides of the tomatoes with the salt and pepper. 3. In a medium-sized bowl, combine the cheese, parsley, onions, garlic, and thyme. Stir to combine well. Divide the mixture evenly among the tomatoes. 4. Spray avocado oil on the tomatoes and place them in the baking pan. Place the tomato tops in the baking pan next to, not on top of, the filled tomatoes. 5. Insert the wire rack into the bottom rack height position. Close the oven door. Turn the FUNCTION dial until the indicator on the LCD screen reaches the BAKE function. Set the temperature to 350°F and set the timer to 15 minutes. Press START/CANCEL to activate. 6. When preheating has completed, place the baking pan on the wire rack and bake for 15 minutes, or until the filling is golden and the tomatoes are soft yet still holding their shape. 7. Garnish with fresh parsley, ground black pepper, and a sprig of basil. Serve warm, with the tomato tops on the vine. 8. Store leftovers in an airtight container in the refrigerator for up to 4 days.

Per Serving: Calories 77; Fat 3.73g; Sodium 378mg; Carbs 7.13g; Fiber 1.5g; Sugar 2.75g; Protein 4.71g

Tasty Roasted Curry Cauliflower

⏱ **Prep: 10 minutes**   🍲 **Cook: 20 minutes**   🍃 **Serves: 4**

Ingredients:

¼ cup olive oil
2 teaspoons curry powder
½ teaspoon salt
¼ teaspoon freshly ground black pepper
1 head cauliflower, cut into bite-size florets
½ red onion, sliced
2 tablespoons freshly chopped parsley, for garnish (optional)

Preparation:

1. In a large bowl, combine the olive oil, curry powder, salt, and pepper. Add the cauliflower and onion. Toss gently until the vegetables are completely coated with the oil mixture. Transfer the vegetables to the baking pan. 2. Insert the wire rack into the bottom rack height position. Close the oven door. Turn the FUNCTION dial until the indicator on the LCD screen reaches the BAKE function. Set the temperature to 400°F and set the timer to 20 minutes. Press START/CANCEL to activate. 3. When preheating has completed, place the baking pan on the wire rack and bake for 20 minutes. Pausing about halfway through the cooking time to shake the pan. Bake until the cauliflower is tender and beginning to brown. 4. Top with the parsley, if desired, before serving.

Per Serving: Calories 145; Fat 13.84g; Sodium 312mg; Carbs 5.23g; Fiber 2.1g; Sugar 1.88g; Protein 1.58g

Prosciutto-Wrapped Asparagus

⏱ **Prep: 10 minutes**　🍲 **Cook: 10 minutes**　🍂 **Serves: 4**

Ingredients:

1-pound asparagus
12 (0.5-ounce) slices prosciutto
1 tablespoon coconut oil, melted
2 teaspoons lemon juice
⅛ teaspoon red pepper flakes
⅓ cup grated Parmesan cheese
2 tablespoons salted butter, melted

Preparation:

1. On a clean work surface, place an asparagus spear onto a slice of prosciutto. 2. Drizzle with coconut oil and lemon juice. Sprinkle red pepper flakes and Parmesan across asparagus. Roll prosciutto around asparagus spear. Place into the baking pan. 3. Insert the wire rack into the bottom rack height position. Close the oven door. Turn the FUNCTION dial until the indicator on the LCD screen reaches the BAKE function. Set the temperature to 375°F and set the timer to 10 minutes. Press START/CANCEL to activate. 4. When preheating has completed, place the baking pan on the wire rack and bake for 10 minutes. 5. Drizzle the asparagus roll with butter before serving.
Per Serving: Calories 190; Fat 13.32g; Sodium 668mg; Carbs 7.38g; Fiber 3g; Sugar 2.21g; Protein 11.95g

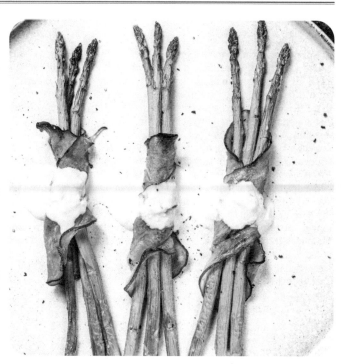

Cheese Bacon Stuffed Sweet Peppers

⏱ **Prep: 15 minutes**　🍲 **Cook: 8 minutes**　🍂 **Serves: 4**

Ingredients:

8 mini sweet peppers
4 ounces full-fat cream cheese, softened
4 slices sugar-free bacon, cooked and crumbled
¼ cup shredded pepper jack cheese

Preparation:

1. Remove the tops from the peppers and slice each one in half lengthwise. Use a small knife to remove their seeds and membranes. 2. In a small bowl, mix together the bacon, cream cheese, and pepper jack. 3. Place 3 teaspoons of the mixture into each sweet pepper and press down smooth. Place on the broiling rack inserted into the baking pan. 4. Insert the wire rack into the bottom rack height position. Close the oven door. Turn the FUNCTION dial until the indicator on the LCD screen reaches the ROAST function. Set the temperature to 400°F and set the timer to 8 minutes. Press START/CANCEL to activate. 5. When preheating has completed, place the baking pan on the wire rack and cook for 8 minutes. Serve warm.
Per Serving: Calories 228; Fat 10.76g; Sodium 329mg; Carbs 25.97g; Fiber 3.3g; Sugar 1.69g; Protein 10.57g

Homemade Bruschetta

⏱ **Prep: 6 minutes**　🍲 **Cook: 8 minutes**　🍃 **Serves: 6**

) **Ingredients:**

1 small tomato, diced
2 tablespoons chopped fresh basil leaves
1 teaspoon dried oregano leaves
¼ teaspoon fine sea salt
3 tablespoons unsalted butter, softened (or olive oil for dairy-free)
1 clove garlic, minced
1 hot dog bun, cut into twelve ½-inch-thick slices
¼ cup plus 2 tablespoons shredded Parmesan cheese

) **Preparation:**

1. Spray the baking pan with avocado oil. 2. In a small bowl, stir together the tomato, basil, oregano, and salt until well combined. Set aside. 3. In another small bowl, mix together the butter and garlic. Spread the garlic butter on one side of each hot dog bun slice. 4. Place the slices in the baking pan buttered side down, spaced about ⅛ inch apart. 5. Insert the wire rack into the bottom rack height position. Close the oven door. Turn the FUNCTION dial until the indicator on the LCD screen reaches the BAKE function. Set the temperature to 360°F and set the timer to 4 minutes. Press START/ CANCEL to activate. 6. When preheating has completed, place the baking pan on the wire rack and bake for 4 minutes. 7. Remove the slices from the oven, flip them so that the buttered side is up, and top each slice with 1½ tablespoons of Parmesan and a dollop of the tomato mixture. 8. Increase the oven temperature to 390°F and return the slices to the oven. Cook for another 2 to 4 minutes, until the bread is crispy and the cheese is melted. 9. Serve immediately and store the slices of bread and the tomato mixture in different airtight containers in the fridge for up to 5 days.
Per Serving: Calories 100; Fat 6.95g; Sodium 172mg; Carbs 7.47g; Fiber 0.4g; Sugar 3.25g; Protein 2.23g

Balsamic Brussels Sprouts with Bacon

⏱ **Prep: 5 minutes**　🍲 **Cook: 12 minutes**　🍃 **Serves: 4**

) **Ingredients:**

2 cups trimmed and halved fresh Brussels sprouts
2 tablespoons olive oil
¼ teaspoon salt
¼ teaspoon ground black pepper
2 tablespoons balsamic vinegar
2 slices cooked sugar-free bacon, crumbled

) **Preparation:**

1. In a large bowl, toss Brussels sprouts with the olive oil, then sprinkle with salt and pepper. Place on the ungreased broiling rack inserted into the baking pan. 2. Insert the wire rack into the bottom rack height position. Close the oven door. Turn the FUNCTION dial until the indicator on the LCD screen reaches the ROAST function. Set the temperature to 375°F and set the timer to 12 minutes. Press START/CANCEL to activate. 3. When preheating has completed, place the baking pan on the wire rack and cook for 12 minutes. 4. Carefully shake the pan halfway through cooking. Brussels sprouts will be tender and browned when done. 5. Place sprouts in a large serving dish and drizzle with balsamic vinegar. Sprinkle bacon over top. Serve warm.
Per Serving: Calories 113; Fat 8.9g; Sodium 255mg; Carbs 5.49g; Fiber 1.7g; Sugar 2.16g; Protein 3.49g

Keto Cauliflower Tots

⏲ Prep: 10 minutes   🍲 Cook: 15 minutes   🍃 Serves: 6

Ingredients:

3 cups cauliflower florets
1 tablespoon coconut flour
1 teaspoon fine sea salt
1 large egg, beaten
1 (8-ounce) package cream cheese (or Kite Hill brand cream cheese style spread for dairy-free), softened
½ cup finely chopped onions
1 teaspoon smoked paprika
Chopped fresh parsley, for garnish (optional)
Ranch Dressing, for serving (optional)

Preparation:

1. Spray the broiling rack with avocado oil. 2. Place the cauliflower in a food processor and pulse until it resembles grains of rice. 3. Place the riced cauliflower in a medium-sized bowl, sprinkle the coconut flour and salt on top, and toss well to coat. Add the egg, cream cheese, onions, and paprika and mix well to combine. 4. Form the cauliflower–cream cheese mixture into 24 tater tot shapes. Place them on the broiling rack inserted into the baking pan, leaving space between them. 5. Insert the wire rack into the bottom rack height position. Close the oven door. Turn the FUNCTION dial until the indicator on the LCD screen reaches the ROAST function. Set the temperature to 400°F and set the timer to 15 minutes. Press START/CANCEL to activate. 6. When preheating has completed, place the baking pan on the wire rack and cook for 15 minutes, or until golden brown. 7. Remove the tots from the oven and place them on a serving plate. Garnish with chopped fresh parsley, if desired, and serve with ranch dressing on the side for dipping, if desired. 8. Store leftovers in an airtight container in the fridge for 3 days or in the freezer for up to a month.
Per Serving: Calories 166; Fat 14.16g; Sodium 560mg; Carbs 6.19g; Fiber 1.8g; Sugar 2.8g; Protein 4.99g

Garlic Butter Cheese Breadsticks

⏲ Prep: 10 minutes   🍲 Cook: 12 minutes   🍃 Serves: 6

Ingredients:

Dough:
1¾ cups shredded mozzarella cheese (about 7 ounces)
2 tablespoons unsalted butter
1 large egg, beaten
¾ cup blanched almond flour
⅛ teaspoon fine sea salt
Garlic Butter:
3 tablespoons unsalted butter, softened
2 cloves garlic, minced
Topping:
½ cup shredded Parmesan cheese (about 2 ounces)
1 teaspoon dried basil leaves
1 teaspoon dried oregano leaves
For Serving (optional):
½ cup marinara sauce

Preparation:

1. Place a piece of parchment paper in a 6-inch square casserole dish and spray it with avocado oil. 2. Make the dough: Place the mozzarella cheese and butter in a microwave-safe bowl and microwave for 1 to 2 minutes, until the cheese is entirely melted. Stir well. Add the egg and, using a hand mixer on low speed, combine well. Add the almond flour and salt and combine well with the hand mixer. 3. Lay a piece of parchment paper on the countertop and place the dough on it. Knead it for about 3 minutes; the dough should be thick yet pliable. (Note: If the dough is too sticky, chill it in the refrigerator for an hour or overnight.) Place the dough in the prepared casserole dish and use your hands to spread it out to fill the bottom of the casserole dish. 4. Make the garlic butter: In a small dish, stir together the butter and garlic until well combined. 5. Spread the garlic butter on top of the dough. Top with the Parmesan, basil, and oregano. 6. Insert the wire rack into the bottom rack height position. Close the oven door. Turn the FUNCTION dial until the indicator on the LCD screen reaches the BAKE function. Set the temperature to 400°F and set the timer to 10 minutes. Press START/CANCEL to activate. 7. When preheating has completed, place the casserole dish on the wire rack and bake for 10 minutes, or until golden brown and cooked through. 8. Cut into 1-inch-wide breadsticks and serve with marinara sauce, if desired. Best served fresh, but leftovers can be stored in an airtight container in the fridge for up to 3 days.
Per Serving: Calories 182; Fat 9.41g; Sodium 446mg; Carbs 6.22g; Fiber 2.3g; Sugar 2.39g; Protein 18.7g

Spicy Chicken Wings

⏱ **Prep: 10 minutes**   🍲 **Cook: 40 minutes**   🍃 **Serves: 4**

Ingredients:

1 tablespoon paprika
1 tablespoon Swerve sugar replacement
½ teaspoon dried oregano
½ teaspoon garlic powder
½ teaspoon freshly ground black pepper
½ teaspoon cayenne
1-pound chicken wings, tips removed

Preparation:

1. In a large bowl, combine the paprika, Swerve, oregano, garlic powder, black pepper, and cayenne. Add the chicken wings and toss until thoroughly coated. Cover and refrigerate for at least 1 hour or up to 8 hours. 2. Working in batches if necessary, arrange the wings in a single layer on the broiling rack inserted into the baking pan. Spray lightly with olive oil. 3. Insert the wire rack into the bottom rack height position. Close the oven door. Turn the FUNCTION dial until the indicator on the LCD screen reaches the ROAST function. Set the temperature to 400°F and set the timer to 40 minutes. Press START/CANCEL to activate. 4. When preheating has completed, place the baking pan on the wire rack and cook for 40 minutes. Pausing halfway through the cooking time to turn the wings. Cook until browned and crispy and a thermometer inserted into the thickest part registers 165°F.

Per Serving: Calories 159; Fat 4.29g; Sodium 93mg; Carbs 3.61g; Fiber 0.8g; Sugar 2.17g; Protein 25.29g

Crispy Cajun-Spiced Kale Chips

⏱ **Prep: 10 minutes**   🍲 **Cook: 10 minutes**   🍃 **Serves: 2**

Ingredients:

1 large bunch kale, stems removed and torn into chip-size pieces (about 6 cups)
2 tablespoons olive oil
1 teaspoon garlic powder
1 teaspoon Creole seasoning

Preparation:

1. In a large bowl, combine the kale, olive oil, garlic powder, and Creole seasoning. Toss until the kale is thoroughly coated. 2. Working in batches, arrange about 2 cups of the kale in an even layer in the baking pan (Allow the mixture to stay as fluffy as possible). 3. Insert the wire rack into the bottom rack height position. Close the oven door. Turn the FUNCTION dial until the indicator on the LCD screen reaches the ROAST function. Set the temperature to 360°F and set the timer to 10 minutes. Press START/CANCEL to activate. 4. When preheating has completed, place the baking pan on the wire rack and cook for 10 minutes. Pausing halfway through to shake the pan. 5. Spread the kale chips on a baking sheet to cool completely. Repeat with the remaining kale. 6. Store in an airtight container at room temperature for up to 2 days.

Per Serving: Calories 228; Fat 15.38g; Sodium 182mg; Carbs 19.56g; Fiber 7.6g; Sugar 4.74g; Protein 8.92g

Delicious Mozzarella Sticks

⏱ **Prep: 10 minutes**   🍲 **Cook: 5 minutes**   ❧ **Serves: 4**

Ingredients:

¼ cup almond flour
¼ cup grated Parmesan cheese
½ teaspoon Italian seasoning
¼ teaspoon garlic powder
1 egg
6 part-skim mozzarella sticks, cut in half

Preparation:

1. In a shallow bowl, combine the almond flour, Parmesan, Italian seasoning, and garlic powder. 2. In a separate shallow bowl, whisk the egg. 3. Working one at a time, dip the mozzarella sticks in the egg wash and then roll in the almond flour mixture, pressing lightly to coat evenly. Arrange the mozzarella sticks on a plate lined with parchment paper. Freeze for 30 minutes. 4. Arrange the mozzarella sticks in a single layer on the broiling rack inserted into the baking pan. Spray generously with olive oil. 5. Insert the wire rack into the bottom rack height position. Close the oven door. Turn the FUNCTION dial until the indicator on the LCD screen reaches the ROAST function. Set the temperature to 400°F and set the timer to 5 minutes. Press START/CANCEL to activate. 6. When preheating has completed, place the baking pan on the wire rack and cook for 5 minutes. Cook until the coating is browned. 7. Let stand for 1 minute before removing to a plate.
Per Serving: Calories 196; Fat 11.26g; Sodium 440mg; Carbs 9.37g; Fiber 0.9g; Sugar 1.06g; Protein 14.52g

Sausage-Stuffed Peppers

⏱ **Prep: 15 minutes**   🍲 **Cook: 30 minutes**   ❧ **Serves: 6**

Ingredients:

Avocado oil spray
8 ounces Italian sausage, casings removed
½ cup chopped mushrooms
¼ cup diced onion
1 teaspoon Italian seasoning
Sea salt
Freshly ground black pepper
1 cup keto-friendly marinara sauce
3 bell peppers, halved and seeded
3 ounces provolone cheese, shredded

Preparation:

1. Spray a large skillet with oil and place it over medium-high heat. Add the sausage and cook for 5 minutes, breaking up the meat with a wooden spoon. Add the mushrooms, onion, and Italian seasoning, and season with salt and pepper. Cook for 5 minutes more. Stir in the marinara sauce and continue cooking until heated through. 2. Scoop the sausage filling into the bell pepper halves. 3. Arrange the peppers in a single layer on the baking pan, working in batches if necessary. Position the wire rack in the top rack height position and place the baking pan on the wire rack. Close the oven door and turn the FUNCTION dial until the indicator on the LCD screen points to BROIL. 4. Set the temperature to 350°F(175°C) with convection turned on and set the timer to 15 minutes. Press the START/CANCEL button to activate. 5. Top the stuffed peppers with the cheese and cook for 3 to 5 minutes more, until the cheese is melted and the peppers are tender. 6. When cooking is complete, serve.
Per Serving: Calories 209; Fat 15.94g; Sodium 937mg; Carbs 6.71g; Fiber 1.4g; Sugar 3.35g; Protein 10.47g

Parmesan Zucchini Fries

⏱ **Prep: 15 minutes**   🍲 **Cook: 10 minutes**   🍃 **Serves: 4**

Ingredients:

2 zucchini
½ cup almond flour
½ cup grated Parmesan cheese
1 teaspoon Italian seasoning
½ teaspoon garlic powder (optional)
Pinch of salt and pepper
1 large egg
1 cup no-sugar-added marinara sauce

Preparation:

1. Slice the zucchini in half lengthwise, then cut into sticks about ½ inch thick and 4 inches long. 2. In a shallow bowl, combine the almond flour, Parmesan, Italian seasoning, garlic powder (if using), salt, and pepper. 3. In another shallow bowl, whisk the egg with a fork until lightly beaten. 4. Dip the zucchini into the egg mixture and then dredge in the almond flour mixture. Arrange in the broiling rack inserted into the baking pan, making sure the pieces do not touch (work in batches if necessary). Generously spray the zucchini with olive oil. 5. Insert the wire rack into the bottom rack height position. Close the oven door. Turn the FUNCTION dial until the indicator on the LCD screen reaches the ROAST function. Set the temperature to 400°F and set the timer to 10 minutes. Press START/CANCEL to activate. 6. When preheating has completed, place the baking pan on the wire rack and cook for 10 minutes. Flip them halfway through the cooking time and spraying with more oil, until crispy. 7. Meanwhile, warm the marinara in the microwave. Serve the zucchini sticks with the marinara sauce.

Per Serving: Calories 150; Fat 5.22g; Sodium 798mg; Carbs 18.99g; Fiber 3.2g; Sugar 3.57g; Protein 8.52g

Parmesan Zucchini Chips

⏱ **Prep: 10 minutes**   🍲 **Cook: 10 minutes**   🍃 **Serves: 6**

Ingredients:

2 large eggs
1 cup finely ground blanched almond flour
½ cup Parmesan cheese
1½ teaspoons sea salt
1 teaspoon garlic powder
½ teaspoon smoked paprika
¼ teaspoon freshly ground black pepper
2 zucchinis, cut into ¼-inch-thick slices
Avocado oil spray

Preparation:

1. Beat the eggs in a shallow bowl. In another bowl, stir together the almond flour, Parmesan cheese, salt, garlic powder, smoked paprika, and black pepper. 2. Dip the zucchini slices in the egg mixture, then coat them with the almond flour mixture. 3. Place the zucchini chips in a single layer on the broiling rack inserted into the baking pan, working in batches if necessary. Spray the chips with oil. 4. Insert the wire rack into the bottom rack height position. Close the oven door. Turn the FUNCTION dial until the indicator on the LCD screen reaches the ROAST function. Set the temperature to 400°F and set the timer to 4 minutes. Press START/CANCEL to activate. 5. When preheating has completed, place the baking pan on the wire rack and cook for 4 minutes. Flip the chips and spray them with more oil. Cook for 4 to 6 minutes more. 6. Serve with your favorite dipping sauce.

Per Serving: Calories 147; Fat 5.4g; Sodium 761mg; Carbs 18.25g; Fiber 2.9g; Sugar 1.82g; Protein 8.02g

Roasted Sweet & Spicy Pecans

⏱ **Prep: 7 minutes**   🍲 **Cook: 15 minutes**   🍃 **Serves: 8**

Ingredients:

3 tablespoons unsalted butter, melted
¼ cup brown sugar substitute, such as Swerve or Sukrin Gold
1½ teaspoons Maldon sea salt (or regular sea salt if you like)
¼ teaspoon cayenne pepper, more or less to taste
2 cups pecan halves

Preparation:

1. Line the baking pan with parchment paper. 2. Place the melted butter in a small pot and whisk in the brown sugar substitute, sea salt, and cayenne pepper. Stir until well combined. 3. Place the pecans in a medium bowl and pour the butter mixture over them. Toss to coat. 4. Place the pecans on the parchment paper in a single layer, working in batches if necessary. 5. Insert the wire rack into the bottom rack height position. Close the oven door. Turn the FUNCTION dial until the indicator on the LCD screen reaches the ROAST function. Set the temperature to 275°F and set the timer to 10 minutes. Press START/CANCEL to activate. 6. When preheating has completed, place the baking pan on the wire rack and cook for 10 minutes. Stir, then cook for 5 minutes more. 7. Transfer the pecans to a parchment paper–lined baking sheet and allow them to cool completely before serving. Store them in an airtight container at room temperature for up to 1 week.
Per Serving: Calories 200; Fat 20.72g; Sodium 442mg; Carbs 4.08g; Fiber 2.4g; Sugar 1.02g; Protein 2.47g

Traditional Scotch Eggs

⏱ **Prep: 10 minutes**   🍲 **Cook: 15 minutes**   🍃 **Serves: 8**

Ingredients:

2 pounds ground pork or ground beef
2 teaspoons fine sea salt
½ teaspoon ground black pepper, plus more for garnish
8 large hard-boiled eggs, peeled
2 cups pork dust
Dijon mustard, for serving (optional)

Preparation:

1. Spray the baking pan with avocado oil. 2. Place the ground pork in a large bowl, add the pepper and salt, and use your hands to mix until seasoned throughout. Flatten about ¼ pound of ground pork in the palm of your hand and place a peeled egg in the center. Fold the pork completely around the egg. Repeat with the remaining eggs. 3. Place the pork dust in a medium-sized bowl. One at a time, roll the ground pork–covered eggs in the pork dust and use your hands to press it into the eggs to form a nice crust. Place the eggs on the baking pan and spray them with avocado oil. 4. Position the wire rack in the top rack height position and place the baking pan on the wire rack. Close the oven door and turn the FUNCTION dial until the indicator on the LCD screen points to BROIL. 5. Set the temperature to 400°F(205°C) with convection turned on and set the timer to 15 minutes. Press the START/CANCEL button to activate. Cook the eggs until the internal temperature of the pork reaches 145°F and the outside is golden brown. 6. Garnish with ground black pepper and serve with Dijon mustard, if desired. 7. Store leftovers in an airtight container in the fridge for up to 7 days or in the freezer for up to a month. Reheat in a preheated 400°F air fryer for 3 minutes, or until heated through.
Per Serving: Calories 380; Fat 22.23g; Sodium 1504mg; Carbs 0.66g; Fiber 0g; Sugar 0.19g; Protein 41.4g

Flavorful Stuffed Peppers

⏱ Prep: 10 minutes   🍲 Cook: 45 minutes   ⊜ Serves: 4

◗ Ingredients:

1 pound 85% lean ground beef
½ yellow onion, chopped
4 bell peppers, tops and seeds removed
1 (10-ounce) package cauliflower "rice," fresh or frozen
½ cup tomato sauce
2 tablespoons chopped fresh parsley
1 teaspoon salt
½ teaspoon freshly ground black pepper
1 cup shredded Cheddar cheese
1 teaspoon fresh chopped dill or parsley, for garnish (optional)

◗ Preparation:

1. Crumble the beef into a single layer on the baking pan. Scatter the onion on top. 2. Position the wire rack in the top rack height position and place the baking pan on the wire rack. Close the oven door and turn the FUNCTION dial until the indicator on the LCD screen points to BROIL. 3. Set the temperature to 400°F(205°C) with convection turned on and set the timer to 20 minutes. Press the START/CANCEL button to activate. 4. Cook for 15 to 20 minutes until the beef is browned and cooked through. 5. Meanwhile, arrange the bell peppers in a microwave-safe dish and cover loosely with parchment paper or plastic wrap. Microwave on high for 2 to 3 minutes until the peppers begin to soften. 6. To assemble the peppers, carefully transfer the beef and onions to a large mixing bowl. Use the side of a spoon to break up any large pieces of beef and drain the grease. 7. To the beef mixture add the cauliflower "rice," salt, tomato sauce, parsley, and black pepper. Stir gently until thoroughly combined. 8. Divide the mixture among the peppers and arrange cut-side up on the baking pan. 9. Place the baking pan on the wire rack and, with the same function, cook at 360°F(180°C) for 15 to 20 minutes until the peppers are soft. Top with the cheese and cook for 1 to 2 minutes longer until melted. 10. When cooking is complete, garnish with herbs if desired, and serve.
Per Serving: Calories 436; Fat 29.75g; Sodium 895mg; Carbs 10.88g; Fiber 3.1g; Sugar 5.55g; Protein 31.92g

Crispy Onion Rings

⏱ Prep: 15 minutes   🍲 Cook: 10 minutes   ⊜ Serves: 6

◗ Ingredients:

1 large sweet onion
1 cup finely ground blanched almond flour
1 cup finely grated Parmesan cheese
1 tablespoon baking powder
1 teaspoon smoked paprika
Sea salt
Freshly ground black pepper
2 large eggs
1 tablespoon heavy (whipping) cream
Avocado oil spray

◗ Preparation:

1. Cut the onion crosswise into ⅓-inch-thick rings. 2. In a medium bowl, combine the almond flour, Parmesan cheese, baking powder, smoked paprika, and salt and pepper to taste. 3. In a separate medium bowl, beat the eggs and heavy cream together. 4. Dip an onion ring in the egg mixture and then into the almond flour mixture. Press the almond flour mixture into the onion. Transfer to a parchment paper–lined baking sheet (I find the parchment helps reduce sticking during prep) and repeat with the remaining onion slices. 5. Arrange the onion rings in a single layer on the broiling rack inserted into the baking pan, working in batches if needed. Spray the onion rings with oil. 6. Insert the wire rack into the bottom rack height position. Close the oven door. Turn the FUNCTION dial until the indicator on the LCD screen reaches the ROAST function. Set the temperature to 350°F and set the timer to 5 minutes. Press START/CANCEL to activate. 7. When preheating has completed, place the baking pan on the wire rack and cook for 5 minutes. 8. Use a spatula to carefully reach under the onions and flip them. Spray the onion rings with oil again and cook for 5 minutes more.
Per Serving: Calories 198; Fat 8.51g; Sodium 410mg; Carbs 22.51g; Fiber 2.9g; Sugar 3.03g; Protein 10.03g

Herbed Chicken Thighs

⏱ **Prep: 5 minutes**   🍲 **Cook: 20 minutes**   🍃 **Serves: 2**

Ingredients:

4 bone-in, skin-on chicken thighs
2 tablespoons unsalted butter, melted
1 teaspoon dried parsley
1 teaspoon dried basil
½ teaspoon garlic powder
¼ teaspoon onion powder
¼ teaspoon dried oregano

Preparation:

1. Brush chicken thighs with butter and sprinkle remaining ingredients over thighs. Place thighs on the broiling rack inserted into the baking pan. 2. Insert the wire rack into the bottom rack height position. Close the oven door. Turn the FUNCTION dial until the indicator on the LCD screen reaches the ROAST function. Set the temperature to 380°F and set the timer to 20 minutes. Press START/CANCEL to activate. 3. When preheating has completed, place the baking pan on the wire rack and cook for 20 minutes. Halfway through the cooking time, flip the thighs. 4. When fully cooked, internal temperature will be at least 165°F and skin will be crispy. Serve warm.
Per Serving: Calories 471; Fat 33.41g; Sodium 758mg; Carbs 1.24g; Fiber 0.3g; Sugar 0.06g; Protein 39.99g

Crispy Parmesan Chicken Breasts

⏱ **Prep: 10 minutes**   🍲 **Cook: 14 minutes**   🍃 **Serves: 4**

Ingredients:

1 pound boneless, skinless chicken breasts
¾ cup dill pickle juice
¾ cup finely ground blanched almond flour
¾ cup finely grated Parmesan cheese
½ teaspoon sea salt
½ teaspoon freshly ground black pepper
2 large eggs
Avocado oil spray

Preparation:

1. Place the chicken breasts in a zip-top bag or between two pieces of plastic wrap. Using a meat mallet, pound the chicken to a uniform ½-inch thickness. 2. Place the chicken in a large bowl with the pickle juice. Cover and allow to brine in the refrigerator for up to 2 hours. 3. In a shallow dish, combine the almond flour, Parmesan cheese, salt, and pepper. In a separate, shallow bowl, beat the eggs. 4. Drain the chicken and pat it dry with paper towels. Dip in the eggs and then in the flour mixture, making sure to press the coating into the chicken. Spray both sides of the coated breasts with oil. 5. Spray the broiling rack with oil and put the chicken inside. Place the broiling rack in the baking pan. 6. Insert the wire rack into the bottom rack height position. Close the oven door. Turn the FUNCTION dial until the indicator on the LCD screen reaches the ROAST function. Set the temperature to 400°F and set the timer to 7 minutes. Press START/CANCEL to activate. 7. When preheating has completed, place the baking pan on the wire rack and cook for 7 minutes. 8. Carefully flip the breasts with a spatula. Spray the breasts again with oil and continue cooking for 6 to 7 minutes more, until golden and crispy.
Per Serving: Calories 353; Fat 9.5g; Sodium 803mg; Carbs 12.56g; Fiber 2g; Sugar 3.87g; Protein 52.89g

Crispy Spicy Chicken Breasts

⏰ **Prep: 15 minutes**   🍲 **Cook: 25 minutes**   🍃 **Serves: 4**

Ingredients:

2 (6-ounce) boneless, skinless chicken breasts
2 tablespoons hot sauce
1 tablespoon chili powder
½ teaspoon cumin
¼ teaspoon onion powder
¼ teaspoon ground black pepper
2 ounces pork rinds, finely ground

Preparation:

1. Slice each chicken breast in half lengthwise. Place the chicken into a large bowl and coat with hot sauce. 2. In a small bowl, mix together the chili powder, onion powder, cumin, and pepper. Sprinkle over chicken. 3. Place the ground pork rinds into a large bowl and dip each piece of chicken into the bowl, coating as much as possible. Place chicken on the broiling rack inserted into the baking pan. 4. Insert the wire rack into the bottom rack height position. Close the oven door. Turn the FUNCTION dial until the indicator on the LCD screen reaches the ROAST function. Set the temperature to 350°F and set the timer to 25 minutes. Press START/CANCEL to activate. 5. When preheating has completed, place the baking pan on the wire rack and cook for 25 minutes. Carefully flip the chicken halfway through the cooking time. 6. When done, internal temperature will be at least 165°F and pork rind coating will be dark golden brown. Serve warm.

Per Serving: Calories 181; Fat 4.97g; Sodium 192mg; Carbs 2.11g; Fiber 1g; Sugar 0.66g; Protein 30.54g

Crispy Pickle Brined Fried Chicken

⏰ **Prep: 7 minutes**   🍲 **Cook: 20 minutes**   🍃 **Serves: 4**

Ingredients:

4 bone-in, skin-on chicken legs, cut into drumsticks and thighs (about 3½ pounds)
Pickle juice from a 24-ounce jar of kosher dill pickles
½ cup flour
Salt and freshly ground black pepper
2 eggs
1 cup fine breadcrumbs
1 teaspoon salt
1 teaspoon freshly ground black pepper
½ teaspoon ground paprika
⅛ teaspoon ground cayenne pepper
Vegetable or canola oil in a spray bottle

Preparation:

1. Place the chicken in a shallow dish and pour the pickle juice over the top. Cover and transfer the chicken to the refrigerator to brine in the pickle juice for 3 to 8 hours. 2. When you are ready to cook, remove the chicken from the refrigerator to let it come to room temperature while you set up a dredging station. Add the flour to a shallow dish and season well with salt and freshly ground black pepper. Stir the eggs in a second shallow dish. In a third shallow dish, combine the breadcrumbs, salt, pepper, paprika and cayenne pepper. 3. Remove the chicken from the pickle brine and gently dry it with a clean kitchen towel. Dredge each piece of chicken in the flour mixture, then dip it into the egg mixture, and finally press it into the breadcrumb mixture to coat all sides of the chicken. Place the breaded chicken on baking pan and spray each piece all over with vegetable oil. 4. Position the wire rack in the bottom rack height position and close the oven door. Turn the FUNCTION dial until the indicator on the LCD screen points to the ROAST function. 5. Set the temperature to 370°F(190°C) with convection turned on and set the timer to 20 minutes. Press the START/CANCEL button to activate. 6. Working in two batches, place two chicken thighs and two drumsticks on the baking pan. 7. When preheating has completed, place the baking pan on the wire rack and roast for 10 minutes. 8. Then, gently turn the chicken pieces over and roast for another 10 minutes. Remove the chicken pieces and let them rest on plate – do not cover. Repeat with the second batch of chicken, cooking for 20 minutes, turning the chicken over halfway through. 9. Lower the temperature to 340(170°C). Place the first batch of chicken on top of the second batch already in the baking pan and cook for an additional 7 minutes. Serve warm and enjoy.

Per Serving: Calories 355; Fat 15.91g; Sodium 2662mg; Carbs 22.21g; Fiber 3g; Sugar 2.82g; Protein 29.81g

Delicious Chicken Enchiladas

⏰ Prep: 20 minutes   🍲 Cook: 10 minutes   🍃 Serves: 4

◗ Ingredients:

1½ cups shredded cooked chicken
⅓ cup low-carb enchilada sauce, divided
½ pound medium-sliced deli chicken
1 cup shredded medium Cheddar cheese
½ cup shredded Monterey jack cheese
½ cup full-fat sour cream
1 medium avocado, peeled, pitted, and sliced

◗ Preparation:

1. In a large bowl, mix shredded chicken and half of the enchilada sauce. Lay slices of deli chicken on a work surface and spoon 2 tablespoons shredded chicken mixture onto each slice. 2. Sprinkle 2 tablespoons of Cheddar onto each roll. Gently roll closed. 3. In a 4-cup round baking dish, place each roll, seam side down. Pour the remaining sauce over the rolls and top with the Monterey jack. 4. Insert the wire rack into the bottom rack height position. Close the oven door. Turn the FUNCTION dial until the indicator on the LCD screen reaches the BAKE function. Set the temperature to 370°F and set the timer to 10 minutes. Press START/CANCEL to activate. 5. When preheating has completed, place the baking dish on the wire rack and cook for 10 minutes. 6. Enchiladas will be golden on top and bubbling when cooked. Serve warm with sour cream and sliced avocado.

Per Serving: Calories 412; Fat 24.79g; Sodium 994mg; Carbs 11.7g; Fiber 3.6g; Sugar 1.48g; Protein 36.43g

Cheese Spinach Stuffed Chicken Breast

⏰ Prep: 15 minutes   🍲 Cook: 25 minutes   🍃 Serves: 2

◗ Ingredients:

1 tablespoon unsalted butter
5 ounces frozen spinach, thawed and drained
½ teaspoon garlic powder, divided
½ teaspoon salt, divided
¼ cup chopped yellow onion
¼ cup crumbled feta
2 (6-ounce) boneless, skinless chicken breasts
1 tablespoon coconut oil

◗ Preparation:

1. In a medium skillet over medium heat, add butter to the pan and sauté spinach 3 minutes. Sprinkle ¼ teaspoon garlic powder and ¼ teaspoon salt onto spinach and add onion to the pan. 2. Continue sautéing 3 more minutes, then remove from heat and place in medium bowl. Fold feta into spinach mixture. 3. Slice a roughly 4" slit into the side of each chicken breast, lengthwise. Spoon half of the mixture into each piece and secure closed with a couple toothpicks. Sprinkle outside of chicken with remaining garlic powder and salt. Drizzle with coconut oil. Place chicken breasts on the broiling rack inserted into the baking pan. 4. Insert the wire rack into the bottom rack height position. Close the oven door. Turn the FUNCTION dial until the indicator on the LCD screen reaches the ROAST function. Set the temperature to 350°F and set the timer to 25 minutes. Press START/CANCEL to activate. 5. When preheating has completed, place the baking pan on the wire rack and cook for 25 minutes. 6. When completely cooked chicken should be golden brown and have an internal temperature of at least 165°F. Slice and serve warm.

Per Serving: Calories 461; Fat 22.31g; Sodium 936mg; Carbs 5.19g; Fiber 2.3g; Sugar 1.73g; Protein 58.47g

Tasty Buffalo Chicken Wings

⏰ Prep: 10 minutes　🍲 Cook: 25 minutes　🍃 Serves: 4

Ingredients:

2 tablespoons baking powder
1 teaspoon smoked paprika
Sea salt
Freshly ground black pepper
2 pounds chicken wings or chicken drumettes
Avocado oil spray
⅓ cup avocado oil
½ cup Buffalo hot sauce, such as Frank's RedHot
¼ cup (4 tablespoons) unsalted butter
2 tablespoons apple cider vinegar
1 teaspoon minced garlic
Blue Cheese Dressing or Garlic Ranch Dressing, for serving

Preparation:

1. In a large bowl, stir together the baking powder, smoked paprika, and salt and pepper to taste. Add the chicken wings and toss to coat. 2. Spray the wings with oil. 3. Place the wings in a single layer on the broiling rack inserted into the baking pan, working in batches if necessary. 4. Insert the wire rack into the bottom rack height position. Close the oven door. Turn the FUNCTION dial until the indicator on the LCD screen reaches the ROAST function. Set the temperature to 400°F and set the timer to 25 minutes. Press START/CANCEL to activate. 5. When preheating has completed, place the baking pan on the wire rack and cook for 25 minutes. 6. Check with an instant-read thermometer and remove when they reach 155°F. Let rest until they reach 165°F. 7. While the wings are cooking, whisk together the avocado oil, hot sauce, butter, vinegar, and garlic in a small saucepan over medium-low heat until warm. 8. When the wings are done cooking, toss them with the Buffalo sauce. Serve warm with the dressing.

Per Serving: Calories 564; Fat 36.93g; Sodium 740mg; Carbs 6.68g; Fiber 1.1g; Sugar 1.51g; Protein 51.01g

Tasty Jerk Chicken Thighs

⏰ Prep: 10 minutes　🍲 Cook: 20 minutes　🍃 Serves: 6

Ingredients:

2 teaspoons ground coriander
1 teaspoon ground allspice
1 teaspoon cayenne pepper
1 teaspoon ground ginger
1 teaspoon salt
1 teaspoon dried thyme
½ teaspoon ground cinnamon
½ teaspoon ground nutmeg
2 pounds chicken thighs, skin on
2 tablespoons vegetable oil

Preparation:

1. In a small bowl, combine the coriander, allspice, ginger, salt, thyme, cayenne, cinnamon, and nutmeg. Stir until thoroughly combined. 2. Arrange the chicken on a 9 × 13-inch baking dish and use paper towels to pat dry. Thoroughly coat both sides of the chicken with the spice mixture. Cover and refrigerate for at least 2 hours, preferably overnight. 3. Position the wire rack in the bottom rack height position and close the oven door. Turn the FUNCTION dial until the indicator on the LCD screen points to the ROAST function. 4. Set the temperature to 360°F(180°C) with convection turned on and set the timer to 20 minutes. Press the START/CANCEL button to activate. 5. Working in batches if necessary, place the chicken in a single layer in the baking pan and lightly coat with the vegetable oil. 6. When preheating has completed, place the baking pan on the wire rack and roast for 15 to 20 minutes, until a thermometer inserted into the thickest part registers 165°F. Pause halfway through the cooking time to flip the chicken. 7. When cooking is complete, serve.

Per Serving: Calories 378; Fat 29.81g; Sodium 511mg; Carbs 1.29g; Fiber 0.4g; Sugar 0.05g; Protein 25.09g

Homemade Rotisserie Chicken

⏱ **Prep: 10 minutes**   🍲 **Cook: 60 minutes**   🌿 **Serves: 8**

Ingredients:

1 (4-pound) chicken, giblets removed
½ onion, quartered
1 tablespoon vegetable oil
Secret Spice Rub:
2 teaspoons salt
1 teaspoon paprika
½ teaspoon onion powder
½ teaspoon garlic powder
½ teaspoon dried thyme
½ teaspoon freshly ground black pepper
¼ teaspoon cayenne

Preparation:

1. Use paper towels to blot the chicken dry. Stuff the chicken with the onion. Rub the chicken with the oil. 2. Make the spice rub by combining the salt, paprika, garlic powder, thyme, onion powder, black pepper, and cayenne in a small bowl and stir until thoroughly combined. Sprinkle the chicken with the spice rub until thoroughly coated. 3. Position the wire rack in the bottom rack height position and close the oven door. Turn the FUNCTION dial until the indicator on the LCD screen points to the ROAST function. 4. Set the temperature to 350°F(175°C) with convection turned on and set the timer to 30 minutes. Press the START/CANCEL button to activate.

5. Place the chicken breast side down in the baking pan. 6. When preheating has completed, place the baking pan on the wire rack and roast. Use tongs to carefully flip the chicken over and roast for an additional 30 minutes, or until the temperature of a thermometer inserted into the thickest part of the chicken registers 165°F. 7. When cooking is complete, let the chicken rest for 10 minutes. Discard the onion and serve.
Per Serving: Calories 508; Fat 35.92g; Sodium 741mg; Carbs 1.23g; Fiber 0.3g; Sugar 0.34g; Protein 42.38g

Indian Tandoori Chicken

⏱ **Prep: 10 minutes**   🍲 **Cook: 20 minutes**   🌿 **Serves: 6**

Ingredients:

¼ cup plain Greek yogurt
2 cloves garlic, minced
1 tablespoon grated fresh ginger
½ teaspoon ground cayenne
½ teaspoon ground turmeric
½ teaspoon garam masala
1 teaspoon ground cumin
1 teaspoon salt
2 pounds boneless chicken thighs, skin on
2 tablespoons chopped fresh cilantro
1 lemon, cut into 6 wedges
½ sweet onion, sliced

Preparation:

1. In a small bowl, combine the ginger, yogurt, cayenne, garlic, turmeric, garam masala, cumin, and salt. Whisk until thoroughly combined. 2. Transfer the yogurt mixture to a large resealable bag. Add the chicken, seal the bag, and massage the bag to ensure chicken is evenly coated. Refrigerate for 1 hour or up to 8 hours. 3. Position the wire rack in the bottom rack height position and close the oven door. Turn the FUNCTION dial until the indicator on the LCD screen points to the ROAST function. 4. Set the temperature to 360°F(180°C) with convection turned on and set the timer to 20 minutes. Press the START/CANCEL button to activate. 5. Remove the chicken from the marinade and discard the marinade. Place the chicken in a single layer in the baking pan. 6. When preheating has completed, place the baking pan on the wire rack and roast for 15 to 20 minutes, until a thermometer inserted into the thickest part registers 165°F. Pause halfway through the cooking time to flip the chicken. 7. When cooking is complete, transfer the chicken to a serving platter. Top with the cilantro and serve with the lemon wedges and sliced onion.
Per Serving: Calories 353; Fat 25.3g; Sodium 516mg; Carbs 4.16g; Fiber 0.5g; Sugar 1.82g; Protein 25.94g

Classic Chicken Parmesan

⏰ **Prep: 10 minutes**   🍲 **Cook: 20 minutes**   ❦ **Serves: 4**

Ingredients:

2 large skinless chicken breasts (about 1¼ pounds)
Salt and freshly ground black pepper
½ cup almond meal
½ cup grated Parmesan cheese
2 teaspoons Italian seasoning
1 egg, lightly beaten
1 tablespoon olive oil
1 cup no-sugar-added marinara sauce
4 slices mozzarella cheese or ½ cup shredded mozzarella

Preparation:

1. Slice the chicken breasts in half horizontally to create 4 thinner chicken breasts. Working with one piece at a time, place the chicken between two pieces of parchment paper and pound with a meat mallet or rolling pin to flatten to an even thickness. Season both sides with the freshly ground black pepper and salt. 2. In a large shallow bowl, combine the Parmesan, almond meal, and Italian seasoning and stir until thoroughly combined. Place the egg in another large shallow bowl. 3. Dip the chicken in the egg, followed by the almond meal mixture, pressing the mixture firmly into the chicken to create an even coating. 4. Position the wire rack in the bottom rack height position and close the oven door. Turn the FUNCTION dial until the indicator on the LCD screen points to the ROAST function. 5. Set the temperature to 360°F(180°C) with convection turned on and set the timer to 20 minutes. Press the START/CANCEL button to activate. 6. Working in batches if necessary, place the chicken in a single layer in the baking pan and coat both sides lightly with vegetable oil. 7. When preheating has completed, place the baking pan on the wire rack and roast for 15 minutes, or until a thermometer inserted into the thickest part registers 165°F. Pause halfway through the cooking time to flip the chicken. 8. Spoon the marinara sauce over each piece of chicken and top with the mozzarella cheese. Roast for an additional 3 to 5 minutes until the cheese is melted. 9. When cooking is complete, serve.
Per Serving: Calories 345; Fat 22.88g; Sodium 495mg; Carbs 10.81g; Fiber 3.4g; Sugar 3.51g; Protein 25.78g

Delicious Turkey Meatballs

⏰ **Prep: 15 minutes**   🍲 **Cook: 10 minutes**   ❦ **Serves: 4**

Ingredients:

1 red bell pepper, seeded and coarsely chopped
2 cloves garlic, coarsely chopped
¼ cup chopped fresh parsley
1½ pounds 85% lean ground turkey
1 egg, lightly beaten
½ cup grated Parmesan cheese
1 teaspoon salt
½ teaspoon freshly ground black pepper

Preparation:

1. In a food processor fitted with a metal blade, combine the bell pepper, garlic, and parsley. Pulse until finely chopped. Transfer the vegetables to a large mixing bowl. 2. Add the turkey, egg, salt, Parmesan, and black pepper. Mix gently until thoroughly combined. Shape the mixture into 1¼-inch meatballs. 3. Position the wire rack in the bottom rack height position and close the oven door. Turn the FUNCTION dial until the indicator on the LCD screen points to the ROAST function. 4. Set the temperature to 400°F(205°C) with convection turned on and set the timer to 10 minutes. Press the START/CANCEL button to activate. 5. Working in batches if necessary, place the meatballs in a single layer in the baking pan and coat lightly with vegetable oil spray. 6. When preheating has completed, place the baking pan on the wire rack and roast for 7 to 10 minutes, until lightly browned and a thermometer inserted into the center of a meatball registers 165°F. Pause halfway through the cooking time to shake the baking pan. 7. When cooking is complete, serve.
Per Serving: Calories 332; Fat 18.81g; Sodium 943mg; Carbs 3.78g; Fiber 0.4g; Sugar 0.69g; Protein 37.25g

Healthy Spinach and Feta Stuffed Chicken Breasts

⏱ Prep: 4 minutes   🍲 Cook: 12 minutes   🍃 Serves: 4

Ingredients:

1 (10-ounce) package frozen spinach, thawed and drained well
1 cup feta cheese, crumbled
½ teaspoon freshly ground black pepper
4 boneless chicken breasts
Salt and freshly ground black pepper
1 tablespoon olive oil

Preparation:

Prepare the filling: 1. Squeeze out as much liquid as possible from the thawed spinach. 2. Rough chop the spinach and transfer it to a mixing bowl with the feta cheese and the freshly ground black pepper.
Prepare the chicken breast: 1. Place the chicken breast on a cutting board and press down on the chicken breast with one hand to keep it stabilized. Make an incision about 1-inch long in the fattest side of the breast. Move the knife up and down inside the chicken breast, without poking through either the top or the bottom, or the other side of the breast. The inside pocket should be about 3-inches long, but the opening should only be about 1-inch wide. If this is too difficult, you can make the incision longer, but you will have to be more careful when cooking the chicken breast since this will expose more of the stuffing. 2. Once you have prepared the chicken breasts, use your fingers to stuff the filling into each pocket, spreading the mixture down as far as you can. 4. Lightly brush or spray the baking pan and the chicken breasts with olive oil. Transfer two of the stuffed chicken breasts to the baking pan. 5. Position the wire rack in the bottom rack height position and close the oven door. Turn the FUNCTION dial until the indicator on the LCD screen points to the ROAST function. 6. Set the temperature to 380°F(195°C) with convection turned on and set the timer to 12 minutes. Press the START/CANCEL button to activate. 7. When preheating has completed, place the baking pan on the wire rack and roast for 12 minutes, flipping the chicken breasts halfway through the cooking time. Remove the chicken to a resting plate and roast the second two breasts for 12 minutes. Return the first batch of chicken to the oven with the second batch and cook for 3 more minutes. When the chicken is cooked, an instant read thermometer should register 165°F in the thickest part of the chicken, as well as in the stuffing. 8. Remove the chicken breasts and let them rest on a cutting board for 2 to 3 minutes. Slice the chicken on the bias and serve with the slices fanned out.
Per Serving: Calories 324; Fat 16.18g; Sodium 1086mg; Carbs 4.82g; Fiber 2.4g; Sugar 1.84g; Protein 41.43g

Delicious Chicken Fajitas

⏱ Prep: 10 minutes   🍲 Cook: 15 minutes   🍃 Serves: 2

Ingredients:

10 ounces boneless, skinless chicken breast, sliced into ¼" strips
2 tablespoons coconut oil, melted
1 tablespoon chili powder
½ teaspoon cumin
½ teaspoon paprika
½ teaspoon garlic powder
¼ medium onion, peeled and sliced
½ medium green bell pepper, seeded and sliced
½ medium red bell pepper, seeded and sliced

Preparation:

1. Place chicken and coconut oil into a large bowl and sprinkle with chili powder, cumin, paprika, and garlic powder. Toss chicken until well coated with seasoning. Place chicken on the broiling rack inserted into the baking pan. 2. Insert the wire rack into the bottom rack height position. Close the oven door. Turn the FUNCTION dial until the indicator on the LCD screen reaches the ROAST function. Set the temperature to 350°F and set the timer to 15 minutes. Press START/CANCEL to activate. 3. When preheating has completed, place the baking pan on the wire rack and cook for 15 minutes. 4. Add onion and peppers into the rack when the timer has 7 minutes remaining. 5. Toss the chicken two or three times during cooking. Vegetables should be tender and chicken fully cooked to at least 165°F internal temperature when finished. Serve warm.
Per Serving: Calories 384; Fat 19.58g; Sodium 224mg; Carbs 6.42g; Fiber 2.9g; Sugar 2.39g; Protein 45.39g

Lemony Garlic Shrimp

⏱ **Prep: 5 minutes**　🍲 **Cook: 6 minutes**　🍃 **Serves: 2**

Ingredients:

1 medium lemon
8 ounces medium shelled and deveined shrimp
2 tablespoons unsalted butter, melted
½ teaspoon Old Bay seasoning
½ teaspoon minced garlic

Preparation:

1. Zest lemon and then cut in half. Place shrimp in a large bowl and squeeze juice from ½ lemon on top of them. 2. Add lemon zest to bowl along with remaining ingredients. Toss shrimp until fully coated. 3. Pour bowl contents on the baking pan. Position the wire rack in the top rack height position and place the baking pan on the wire rack. Close the oven door and turn the FUNCTION dial until the indicator on the LCD screen points to BROIL. 4. Set the temperature to 400°F(205°C) with convection turned on and set the timer to 6 minutes. Press the START/CANCEL button to activate. 5. Shrimp will be bright pink when fully cooked. Serve warm with pan sauce.

Per Serving: Calories 173; Fat 8.37g; Sodium 140mg; Carbs 2g; Fiber 0.1g; Sugar 0.61g; Protein 23.4g

Simple Blackened Shrimp

⏱ **Prep: 5 minutes**　🍲 **Cook: 6 minutes**　🍃 **Serves: 2**

Ingredients:

8 ounces medium shrimp
2 tablespoons salted butter, melted
1 teaspoon paprika
½ teaspoon garlic powder
¼ teaspoon onion powder
½ teaspoon Old Bay seasoning

Preparation:

1. Toss all ingredients together in a large bowl. 2. Place the shrimps on the baking pan. Position the wire rack in the top rack height position and place the baking pan on the wire rack. Close the oven door and turn the FUNCTION dial until the indicator on the LCD screen points to BROIL. 3. Set the temperature to 400°F(205°C) with convection turned on and set the timer to 6 minutes. Press the START/CANCEL button to activate. 4. Turn the shrimp halfway through the cooking time to ensure even cooking. 5. When cooking is complete, serve immediately.

Per Serving: Calories 171; Fat 8.37g; Sodium 198mg; Carbs 1.56g; Fiber 0.6g; Sugar 0.16g; Protein 23.21g

Fish Street Tacos with Sriracha Slaw

⏲ Prep: 10 minutes   🍴 Cook: 5 minutes   🍃 Serves: 5-6

Ingredients:

Sriracha Slaw:
½ cup mayonnaise
2 tablespoons rice vinegar
1 teaspoon sugar
2 tablespoons sriracha chili sauce
5 cups shredded purple cabbage
¼ cup shredded carrots
2 scallions, chopped
Salt and freshly ground black pepper
Tacos:
½ cup flour
1 teaspoon chili powder
½ teaspoon ground cumin
1 teaspoon salt
Freshly ground black pepper
½ teaspoon baking powder
1 egg, beaten
¼ cup milk
1 cup breadcrumbs
1 pound mahi-mahi or snapper fillets
1 tablespoon canola or vegetable oil
6 (6-inch) flour tortillas
1 lime, cut into wedges

Preparation:

1. Make the sriracha slaw by combining the mayonnaise, sugar, rice vinegar, and sriracha sauce in a large bowl. Mix well and add the carrots, purple cabbage, and scallions. Toss until all the vegetables are coated with the dressing and season with pepper and salt. Refrigerate the slaw until you are ready to serve the tacos. 2. Combine the flour, salt, cumin, pepper, chili powder, and baking powder in a bowl. Add the egg and milk to mix until the batter is smooth. Add the breadcrumbs to shallow dish. 3. Cut the fish fillets into 1-inch wide sticks, approximately 4-inches long. There will be about 12 fish sticks total. Dredge the fish sticks into the batter, coating all sides. Allow the excess batter to drip off the fish and roll them in the breadcrumbs, patting the crumbs onto all sides of the fish sticks. Arrange the coated fish on a plate or baking sheet until all the fish has been coated. 4. Brush the coated fish sticks with oil on all sides. Spray or brush the baking pan with oil and transfer the fish to the baking pan, leaving a little room around each stick. 5. Position the wire rack in the top rack height position and place the baking pan on the wire rack. Close the oven door and turn the FUNCTION dial until the indicator on the LCD screen points to BROIL. 6. Set the temperature to 400°F(205°C) with convection turned on and set the timer to 3 minutes. Press the START/CANCEL button to activate. 7. Turn the fish sticks over and cook for an additional 2 minutes. 8. While the fish is cooking, warm the tortilla shells wrapped in foil either in a 350°F air fryer or in a skillet with a little oil over medium-high heat for a couple minutes. Fold the tortillas in half and keep them warm until the remaining tortillas and fish are ready. 9. To assemble the tacos, arrange two pieces of the fish in each tortilla shell and top with sriracha slaw. Squeeze lime wedge over top and dig in.
Per Serving: Calories 370; Fat 12.76g; Sodium 615mg; Carbs 40.79g; Fiber 5.1g; Sugar 6.24g; Protein 23.11g

Crispy Coconut Shrimp

⏲ Prep: 5 minutes   🍴 Cook: 6 minutes   🍃 Serves: 2

Ingredients:

8 ounces medium shelled and deveined shrimp
2 tablespoons salted butter, melted
½ teaspoon Old Bay seasoning
¼ cup unsweetened shredded coconut

Preparation:

1. In a large bowl, toss the shrimp in butter and Old Bay seasoning. 2. Place shredded coconut in bowl. Coat each piece of shrimp in the coconut and place on the baking pan. Position the wire rack in the top rack height position and place the baking pan on the wire rack. Close the oven door and turn the FUNCTION dial until the indicator on the LCD screen points to BROIL. 3. Set the temperature to 400°F(205°C) with convection turned on and set the timer to 6 minutes. Press the START/CANCEL button to activate. 4. Gently turn the shrimp halfway through the cooking time. 5. When cooking is complete, serve immediately.
Per Serving: Calories 200; Fat 11.56g; Sodium 199mg; Carbs 1.64g; Fiber 0.9g; Sugar 0.63g; Protein 23.22g

Fish Sticks with Tartar Sauce

⏱ **Prep: 10 minutes**   🍳 **Cook: 15 minutes**   🍃 **Serves: 4**

Ingredients:

1½ pounds cod fillets, cut into 1-inch strips
1 teaspoon salt
½ teaspoon freshly ground black pepper
2 eggs
¾ cup almond flour
¼ cup grated Parmesan cheese
Tartar Sauce:
½ cup sour cream
½ cup mayonnaise
3 tablespoons chopped dill pickle
2 tablespoons capers, drained and chopped
½ teaspoon dried dill
1 tablespoon dill pickle liquid (optional)

Preparation:

1. Season the cod with the black pepper and salt and set aside. 2. In a shallow bowl, lightly beat the eggs. In a second shallow bowl, combine the almond flour and Parmesan cheese. Stir until thoroughly combined. 3. Working with a few pieces at a time, dip the fish into the egg mixture followed by the flour mixture. Press lightly to ensure an even coating. 4. Working in batches if necessary, arrange the fish in a single layer in the baking pan and spray lightly with olive oil. 5. Position the wire rack in the top rack height position and place the baking pan on the wire rack. Close the oven door and turn the FUNCTION dial until the indicator on the LCD screen points to BROIL. 6. Set the temperature to 400°F(205°C) with convection turned on and set the timer to 15 minutes. Press the START/CANCEL button to activate. Broil for 12 to 15 minutes, until the fish flakes easily with a fork. Pause halfway through the cooking time to turn the fish. 5. When cooking is complete, let sit in the pan for a few minutes before serving with the tartar sauce. 6. Make the tartar sauce by combining the sour cream, mayonnaise, pickle, capers, and dill in a small bowl. If you prefer a thinner sauce, stir in the pickle liquid.
Per Serving: Calories 400; Fat 17.45g; Sodium 1599mg; Carbs 22.65g; Fiber 1.3g; Sugar 0.56g; Protein 35.95g

Savory Sesame-Crusted Salmon

⏱ **Prep: 10 minutes**   🍳 **Cook: 10 minutes**   🍃 **Serves: 4**

Ingredients:

¼ cup mixed black and brown sesame seeds
1 tablespoon reduced-sodium soy sauce
1 teaspoon sesame oil
1 teaspoon honey
4 (6-ounce) salmon filets, skin removed
2 tablespoons chopped fresh marjoram, for garnish (optional)

Preparation:

1. Place the sesame seeds on a plate or in a small shallow bowl. In a separate small bowl, combine the soy sauce, sesame oil, and honey. 2. Brush all sides of the salmon with the soy sauce mixture until thoroughly coated. Press the top of each filet into the sesame seeds to create a coating. 3. Arrange the fish in a single layer in the baking pan, seed-side up. 4. Position the wire rack in the top rack height position and place the baking pan on the wire rack. Close the oven door and turn the FUNCTION dial until the indicator on the LCD screen points to BROIL. 5. Set the temperature to 360°F(180°C) with convection turned on and set the timer to 10 minutes. Press the START/CANCEL button to activate. Broil for 10 minutes until the fish is firm and flakes easily with a fork. 6. Top with the marjoram, if desired, before serving.
Per Serving: Calories 133; Fat 8.81g; Sodium 165mg; Carbs 3.28g; Fiber 1.5g; Sugar 1.56g; Protein 11.07g

Tuna Patties with Spicy Sriracha Sauce

⏱ Prep: 10 minutes   🍳 Cook: 10 minutes   🍽 Serves: 4

Ingredients:

2 (6-ounce) cans tuna packed in oil, drained
3 tablespoons almond flour
2 tablespoons mayonnaise
1 teaspoon dried dill
½ teaspoon onion powder
Pinch of salt and pepper
Spicy Sriracha Sauce:
¼ cup mayonnaise
1 tablespoon sriracha sauce
1 teaspoon garlic powder

Preparation:

1. Line the baking pan with parchment paper. 2. In a large bowl, combine the almond flour, tuna, dill, mayonnaise, and onion powder. Season to taste with freshly ground black pepper and salt. Use a fork to stir, mashing with the back of the fork as necessary, until thoroughly combined. 3. Form the tuna mixture patties with an ice cream scoop. Place the patties in a single layer on the parchment paper in the baking pan. Press lightly with the bottom of the scoop to flatten into a circle about ½ inch thick. 4. Position the wire rack in the top rack height position and place the baking pan on the wire rack. Close the oven door and turn the FUNCTION dial until the indicator on the LCD screen points to BROIL. 5. Set the temperature to 380°F(195°C) with convection turned on and set the timer to 10 minutes. Broil until lightly browned. Press the START/CANCEL button to activate. Pause halfway through the cooking time to turn the patties. 6. To make the sriracha sauce by combining the mayonnaise, sriracha, and garlic powder in a small bowl. 7. When cooking is complete, serve the tuna patties topped with the sriracha sauce.
Per Serving: Calories 154; Fat 7.71g; Sodium 515mg; Carbs 8.99g; Fiber 1g; Sugar 1.12g; Protein 12.43g

Sea Scallops with Lemon-Butter Sauce

⏱ Prep: 5 minutes   🍳 Cook: 15 minutes   🍽 Serves: 4

Ingredients:

1 pound large sea scallops
Sea salt
Freshly ground black pepper
Avocado oil spray
¼ cup (4 tablespoons) unsalted butter
1 tablespoon freshly squeezed lemon juice
1 teaspoon minced garlic
¼ teaspoon red pepper flakes

Preparation:

1. If your scallops still have the adductor muscles attached, remove them. Pat the scallops dry with a paper towel. 2. Season the scallops with pepper and salt, then place them on a plate and refrigerate for 15 minutes. 3. Spray the baking pan with oil, and arrange the scallops in a single layer. Spray the top of the scallops with oil. 4. Position the wire rack in the top rack height position and place the baking pan on the wire rack. Close the oven door and turn the FUNCTION dial until the indicator on the LCD screen points to BROIL. 5. Set the temperature to 350°F(175°C) with convection turned on and set the timer to 6 minutes. Press the START/CANCEL button to activate. 6. Flip the scallops and cook for 6 minutes more, until an instant-read thermometer reads 145°F. 7. While the scallops cook, place the butter, garlic, lemon juice, and red pepper flakes in a small ramekin. 8. When the scallops have finished cooking, remove them from the oven. Place the ramekin in the oven and cook until the butter melts, about 3 minutes. Stir. 9. Toss the scallops with the warm butter and serve.
Per Serving: Calories 202; Fat 8.95g; Sodium 1053mg; Carbs 7.07g; Fiber 0.1g; Sugar 0.26g; Protein 23.9g

Fresh Coconut Shrimp

⏰ **Prep:** 15 minutes   🍲 **Cook:** 17 minutes   🍃 **Serves:** 4

Ingredients:

¾ cup unsweetened shredded coconut
¾ cup coconut flour
1 teaspoon garlic powder
¼ teaspoon cayenne pepper
Sea salt
Freshly ground black pepper
2 large eggs
1 pound fresh extra-large or jumbo shrimp, peeled and deveined
Avocado oil spray

Preparation:

1. In a medium bowl, combine the shredded coconut, garlic powder, coconut flour, and cayenne pepper. Season to taste with pepper and salt. 2. In a small bowl, beat the eggs. 3. Pat the shrimp dry with paper towels. Dip each shrimp in the eggs and then the coconut mixture. Gently press the coating to the shrimp to help it adhere. 4. Spray the shrimp with oil and place them in a single layer on the baking pan, working in batches if necessary. 5. Position the wire rack in the top rack height position and place the baking pan on the wire rack. Close the oven door and turn the FUNCTION dial until the indicator on the LCD screen points to BROIL. 6. Set the temperature to 400°F(205°C) with convection turned on and set the timer to 9 minutes. Press the START/CANCEL button to activate. 7. Cook the shrimp for 9 minutes, then flip and spray them with more oil. Cook for 8 minutes more, until the center of the shrimp is opaque and cooked through. 6. When cooking is complete, serve with sauce if desired.

Per Serving: Calories 234; Fat 9.53g; Sodium 555mg; Carbs 10.99g; Fiber 1.5g; Sugar 8.83g; Protein 26.93g

Sweet and Spicy Salmon Fillets

⏰ **Prep:** 5 minutes   🍲 **Cook:** 12 minutes   🍃 **Serves:** 4

Ingredients:

½ cup sugar-free mayonnaise (homemade, or store-bought)
2 tablespoons brown sugar substitute, such as Sukrin Gold
2 teaspoons Dijon mustard
1 canned chipotle chile in adobo sauce, diced
1 teaspoon adobo sauce (from the canned chipotle)
16 ounces salmon fillets
Salt
Freshly ground black pepper

Preparation:

1. In a small food processor, mix up the mayonnaise, Dijon mustard, brown sugar substitute, chipotle pepper, and adobo sauce. Process for 1 minute until everything is combined and the brown sugar substitute is no longer granular. 2. Season the salmon with pepper and salt. Spread half of the sauce over the fish, and reserve the remainder of the sauce for serving. 3. Place the salmon on the baking pan. Position the wire rack in the top rack height position and place the baking pan on the wire rack. Close the oven door and turn the FUNCTION dial until the indicator on the LCD screen points to BROIL. 4. Set the temperature to 400°F(205°C) with convection turned on and set the timer to 5 minutes. Press the START/CANCEL button to activate. 5. Flip the salmon and cook for 5 to 7 minutes more, until an instant-read thermometer reads 125°F (for medium-rare). 6. When cooking is complete, serve warm with the remaining sauce.

Per Serving: Calories 245; Fat 14.03g; Sodium 791mg; Carbs 4.79g; Fiber 0.7g; Sugar 2.38g; Protein 23.67g

Garlic Butter Shrimp

⏱ Prep: 5 minutes   🍴 Cook: 10 minutes   ⬗ Serves: 4

Ingredients:

1 pound fresh large shrimp, peeled and deveined
1 tablespoon avocado oil
2 teaspoons minced garlic, divided
½ teaspoon red pepper flakes
Sea salt
Freshly ground black pepper
2 tablespoons unsalted butter, melted
2 tablespoons chopped fresh parsley

Preparation:

1. Place the shrimp in a large bowl and toss with the avocado oil, 1 teaspoon of minced garlic, and red pepper flakes. Season with pepper and salt. 2. Arrange the shrimp in a single layer on the baking pan, working in batches if necessary. 3. Position the wire rack in the top rack height position and place the baking pan on the wire rack. Close the oven door and turn the FUNCTION dial until the indicator on the LCD screen points to BROIL. 4. Set the temperature to 350°F(175°C) with convection turned on and set the timer to 6 minutes. Press the START/CANCEL button to activate. 5. Turn the shrimp over and cook for 2 to 4 minutes more, until the internal temperature of the shrimp reaches 120°F. 6. While the shrimp are cooking, melt the butter in a small saucepan over medium heat and add the remaining 1 teaspoon of garlic to stir. 7. When cooking is complete, transfer the cooked shrimp to a large skillet, add the garlic butter, and toss well. Top with the parsley and serve warm.

Per Serving: Calories 168; Fat 7.98g; Sodium 430mg; Carbs 1.31g; Fiber 0.3g; Sugar 0.32g; Protein 23.31g

Crispy Fish Sticks

⏱ Prep: 15 minutes   🍴 Cook: 10 minutes   ⬗ Serves: 4

Ingredients:

1 ounce pork rinds, finely ground
¼ cup blanched finely ground almond flour
½ teaspoon Old Bay seasoning
1 tablespoon coconut oil
1 large egg
1 pound cod fillet, cut into ¾" strips

Preparation:

1. Place ground pork rinds, Old Bay seasoning, almond flour, and coconut oil into a large bowl and mix together. In a medium bowl, whisk egg. 2. Dip each fish stick into the egg and then gently press into the flour mixture, coating as fully and evenly as possible. Place fish sticks on the baking pan. Position the wire rack in the top rack height position and place the baking pan on the wire rack. Close the oven door and turn the FUNCTION dial until the indicator on the LCD screen points to BROIL. 3. Set the temperature to 400°F(205°C) with convection turned on and set the timer to 10 minutes. Press the START/CANCEL button to activate. Cook until golden. 4. When cooking is complete, serve immediately with sauce if desired.

Per Serving: Calories 169; Fat 5.81g; Sodium 366mg; Carbs 6.12g; Fiber 0.2g; Sugar 0.07g; Protein 21.67g

Balsamic-Maple Glazed Salmon

⏲ Prep: 5 minutes 　 🍲 Cook: 10 minutes 　 ❧ Serves: 4

Ingredients:

4 (6-ounce) fillets of salmon
Salt and freshly ground black pepper
Vegetable oil
¼ cup pure maple syrup
3 tablespoons balsamic vinegar
1 teaspoon Dijon mustard

Preparation:

1. Season the salmon well with freshly ground black pepper and salt. Spray or brush the bottom of the baking pan with vegetable oil and place the salmon fillets inside. 2. Position the wire rack in the top rack height position and place the baking pan on the wire rack. Close the oven door and turn the FUNCTION dial until the indicator on the LCD screen points to BROIL. 3. Set the temperature to 400°F(205°C) with convection turned on and set the timer to 5 minutes. Press the START/CANCEL button to activate. 4. While the salmon is cooking, add the balsamic vinegar, maple syrup, and Dijon mustard in a small saucepan over medium heat and stir to blend well. Let the mixture simmer while the fish is cooking. It should start to thicken slightly, but keep your eye on it so it doesn't burn. 5. Brush the glaze on the salmon fillets and cook for an additional 5 minutes. 6. The salmon should feel firm to the touch when finished and the glaze should be nicely browned on top. Brush a little more glaze on top before removing, garnish with the sesame seeds if desired, and serving with rice and vegetables, or a nice green salad.
Per Serving: Calories 116; Fat 1.92g; Sodium 331mg; Carbs 15.52g; Fiber 0.1g; Sugar 13.72g; Protein 8.71g

Homemade Bang Bang Shrimp

⏲ Prep: 15 minutes 　 🍲 Cook: 14 minutes 　 ❧ Serves: 4

Ingredients:

For the Sauce:
½ cup mayonnaise
¼ cup sweet chili sauce
2 to 4 tablespoons sriracha
1 teaspoon minced fresh ginger
For the Shrimp:
1 pound jumbo raw shrimp (21 to 25 count), peeled and deveined
2 tablespoons cornstarch or rice flour
½ teaspoon kosher salt
Vegetable oil spray
For the sauce: 1. In a large bowl, combine the sriracha, mayonnaise, chili sauce, and ginger. Stir until well combined. Remove half of the sauce to serve as a dipping sauce.
For the shrimp: 1. Place the shrimp in a medium bowl. Sprinkle the cornstarch and salt over the shrimp and toss until well coated. 2. Place the shrimp on the baking pan in a single layer. Spray generously with vegetable oil spray. 3. Position the wire rack in the top rack height position and place the baking pan on the wire rack. Close the oven door and turn the FUNCTION dial until the indicator on the LCD screen points to BROIL. 4. Set the temperature to 350°F(175°C) with convection turned on and set the timer to 10 minutes. Press the START/CANCEL button to activate. 5. Turn and spray with additional oil spray halfway through the cooking time. 6. Remove the shrimp and toss in the bowl with half of the sauce. Place the shrimp back in the oven. Continue to cook at 350°F(175°C) for an additional 4 to 5 minutes, or until the sauce has formed a glaze. 7. When cooking is complete, serve the hot shrimp with the reserved sauce for dipping.
Per Serving: Calories 205; Fat 6.47g; Sodium 689mg; Carbs 12.84g; Fiber 1.2g; Sugar 3.86g; Protein 23.84g

Easy Ginger-Scallion Fish

🕐 **Prep:** 15 minutes   🍲 **Cook:** 15 minutes   🍃 **Serves:** 2

Ingredients:

For the Bean Sauce:
2 tablespoons soy sauce
1 tablespoon rice wine
1 tablespoon doubanjiang (Chinese black bean paste)
1 teaspoon minced fresh ginger
1 clove garlic, minced
For the Vegetables and Fish:
1 tablespoon peanut oil
¼ cup julienned green onions (white and green parts)
¼ cup chopped fresh cilantro
2 tablespoons julienned fresh ginger
2 (6-ounce) white fish fillets, such as tilapia

For the sauce: 1. In a small bowl, combine all the ingredients and stir until well combined; set aside.
For the vegetables and fish: 1. In a medium bowl, combine the cilantro, peanut oil, green onions, and ginger. Toss to combine. 2. Cut two squares of parchment large enough to hold one fillet and half of the vegetables. Place one fillet on each parchment square, top with the vegetables, and pour over the sauce. Fold over the parchment paper and crimp the sides in small, tight folds to hold the fish, vegetables, and sauce securely inside the packet. 3. Place the packets in a single layer on the baking pan. Position the wire rack in the top rack height position and place the baking pan on the wire rack. Close the oven door and turn the FUNCTION dial until the indicator on the LCD screen points to BROIL. 4. Set the temperature to 350°F(175°C) with convection turned on and set the timer to 15 minutes. Press the START/CANCEL button to activate. 5. When cooking is complete, transfer each packet to a dinner plate. Cut open with scissors just before serving.
Per Serving: Calories 201; Fat 8.89g; Sodium 942mg; Carbs 8.14g; Fiber 1.4g; Sugar 3.24g; Protein 22.1g

Pork Tenderloin with Avocado Lime Sauce

⏰ **Prep: 10 minutes**   🍲 **Cook: 15 minutes**   ❧ **Serves: 4**

Ingredients:

Marinade:
½ cup lime juice
Grated zest of 1 lime
2 teaspoons stevia glycerite, or ¼ teaspoon liquid stevia
3 cloves garlic, minced
1½ teaspoons fine sea salt
1 teaspoon chili powder, or more for more heat
1 teaspoon smoked paprika
1 pound pork tenderloin
Avocado Lime Sauce:
1 medium-sized ripe avocado, roughly chopped
½ cup full-fat sour cream (or coconut cream for dairy-free)
Grated zest of 1 lime
Juice of 1 lime
2 cloves garlic, roughly chopped
½ teaspoon fine sea salt
¼ teaspoon ground black pepper
Chopped fresh cilantro leaves, for garnish
Lime slices, for serving
Pico de gallo, for serving

Preparation:

1. In a medium-sized casserole dish, stir together all the marinade
ingredients until well combined. Add the tenderloin and coat it well in the marinade. Cover and place in the fridge to marinate for 2 hours or overnight. 2. Spray the baking pan with avocado oil. 3. Remove the pork from the marinade and place it on the baking pan. Position the wire rack in the top rack height position and place the baking pan on the wire rack. Close the oven door and turn the FUNCTION dial until the indicator on the LCD screen points to BROIL. 4. Set the temperature to 400°F(205°C) with convection turned on and set the timer to 15 minutes. Press the START/CANCEL button to activate. Cook until the internal temperature of the pork is 145°F, flipping after 7 minutes. 5. Remove the pork from the baking pan and place it on a cutting board. Let it rest for 8 to 10 minutes and then cut it into ½-inch-thick slices. 6. While the pork cooks, make the avocado lime sauce by placing all the sauce ingredients in a food processor and puree until smooth. Taste and adjust the seasoning to your liking. 7. Place the pork slices on a serving platter and spoon the avocado lime sauce on top. Garnish with the cilantro leaves and serve with the lime slices and pico de gallo. 7. Store leftovers in an airtight container in the fridge for up to 4 days. Reheat in a preheated 400°F air fryer for 5 minutes, or until heated through.
Per Serving: Calories 290; Fat 11.59g; Sodium 1293mg; Carbs 18.75g; Fiber 4.2g; Sugar 1.8g; Protein 32.31g

Barbecued Pork Riblets

⏱ Prep: 10 minutes 🍲 Cook: 25 minutes ❧ Serves: 4

Ingredients:

1 rack pork riblets, cut into individual riblets
1 teaspoon fine sea salt
1 teaspoon ground black pepper
Sauce:
¼ cup apple cider vinegar
¼ cup beef broth
¼ cup Swerve confectioners'-style sweetener or equivalent amount of liquid or powdered sweetener
¼ cup tomato sauce
1 teaspoon liquid smoke
1 teaspoon onion powder
2 cloves garlic, minced

Preparation:

1. Spray the baking pan with avocado oil. 2. Season the riblets well on all sides with the pepper and salt. Place the riblets on the baking pan. Position the wire rack in the top rack height position and place the baking pan on the wire rack. Close the oven door and turn the FUNCTION dial until the indicator on the LCD screen points to BROIL. 3. Set the temperature to 350˚F(175˚C) with convection turned on and set the timer to 20 minutes. Press the START/CANCEL button to activate. Flip halfway through. 4. While the riblets cook, mix all the sauce ingredients together in a 6-inch pie pan that fits into your appliance. 5. Remove the riblets from the baking pan and place them in the pie pan with the sauce. Stir to coat the riblets in the sauce. Transfer the pan to the oven and cook for 10 to 15 minutes, until the pork is cooked through and the internal temperature reaches 145°F. 6. Store leftovers in an airtight container in the refrigerator for up to 4 days. Reheat in a preheated 350°F air fryer for 5 minutes, or until heated through.
Per Serving: Calories 265; Fat 6.76g; Sodium 988mg; Carbs 8.36g; Fiber 1.6g; Sugar 3.35g; Protein 40.03g

Spicy Baby Back Ribs

⏱ Prep: 5 minutes 🍲 Cook: 35 minutes ❧ Serves: 2

Ingredients:

2 teaspoons fine sea salt
1 teaspoon ground black pepper
2 teaspoons smoked paprika
1 teaspoon garlic powder
1 teaspoon onion powder
½ teaspoon chili powder (optional, for a spicy kick)
1 rack baby back ribs, cut in half crosswise

Preparation:

1. Spray the baking pan with avocado oil. 2. In a small bowl, combine the pepper, salt, and seasonings. Season the ribs on all sides with the seasoning mixture. 3. Place the ribs on the baking pan. Position the wire rack in the top rack height position and place the baking pan on the wire rack. Close the oven door and turn the FUNCTION dial until the indicator on the LCD screen points to BROIL. 4. Set the temperature to 350˚F(175˚C) with convection turned on and set the timer to 20 minutes. Press the START/CANCEL button to activate. 5. Then flip the ribs over and cook for another 15 to 20 minutes, until the ribs are cooked through and the internal temperature reaches 145°F. 6. Store leftovers in an airtight container in the refrigerator for up to 4 days. Reheat in a preheated 350°F air fryer for 5 minutes, or until heated through.
Per Serving: Calories 296; Fat 10.16g; Sodium 2471mg; Carbs 4.59g; Fiber 1.7g; Sugar 0.41g; Protein 44.97g

Beef and Broccoli Stir-Fry

⏰ Prep: 5 minutes   🍲 Cook: 20 minutes   🍃 Serves: 2

Ingredients:

½ pound sirloin steak, thinly sliced
2 tablespoons soy sauce (or liquid aminos)
¼ teaspoon grated ginger
¼ teaspoon finely minced garlic
1 tablespoon coconut oil
2 cups broccoli florets
¼ teaspoon crushed red pepper
⅛ teaspoon xanthan gum
½ teaspoon sesame seeds

Preparation:

1. To marinate beef, place it into a large bowl or storage bag and add soy sauce, ginger, garlic, and coconut oil. Allow to marinate for 1 hour in refrigerator. 2. Remove beef from marinade, reserving marinade, and place beef on the baking pan. Position the wire rack in the top rack height position and place the baking pan on the wire rack. Close the oven door and turn the FUNCTION dial until the indicator on the LCD screen points to BROIL. 3. Set the temperature to 320°F(160°C) with convection turned on and set the timer to 20 minutes. Press the START/CANCEL button to activate. 4. After 10 minutes, add broccoli and sprinkle red pepper into the baking pan and shake. 5. Pour the marinade into a skillet over medium heat and bring to a boil, then reduce to simmer. Stir in xanthan gum and allow to thicken. 6. When cooking is complete, quickly empty the baking pan into skillet and toss. Sprinkle with sesame seeds. Serve immediately.

Per Serving: Calories 295; Fat 20.09g; Sodium 585mg; Carbs 2.2g; Fiber 1.3g; Sugar 0.25g; Protein 26.18g

Tender Peppercorn-Crusted Beef Tenderloin

⏰ Prep: 10 minutes   🍲 Cook: 25 minutes   🍃 Serves: 6

Ingredients:

2 tablespoons salted butter, melted
2 teaspoons minced roasted garlic
3 tablespoons ground 4-peppercorn blend
1 (2-pound) beef tenderloin, trimmed of visible fat

Preparation:

1. In a small bowl, combine the butter and roasted garlic. Brush it over the beef tenderloin. 2. Place the ground peppercorns onto a plate and roll the tenderloin through them, creating a crust. Place tenderloin on the baking pan. Position the wire rack in the top rack height position and place the baking pan on the wire rack. Close the oven door and turn the FUNCTION dial until the indicator on the LCD screen points to BROIL. 3. Set the temperature to 400°F(205°C) with convection turned on and set the timer to 25 minutes. Press the START/CANCEL button to activate. 4. Turn the tenderloin halfway through the cooking time. 5. When cooking is complete, allow meat to rest 10 minutes before slicing.

Per Serving: Calories 352; Fat 16.13g; Sodium 108mg; Carbs 2.52g; Fiber 0.9g; Sugar 0.03g; Protein 46.56

Mouthwatering Lasagna Casserole

⏲ Prep: 15 minutes   🍲 Cook: 15 minutes   🍲 Serves: 4

Ingredients:

¾ cup low-carb no-sugar-added pasta sauce
1 pound 80/20 ground beef, cooked and drained
½ cup full-fat ricotta cheese
¼ cup grated Parmesan cheese
½ teaspoon garlic powder
1 teaspoon dried parsley
½ teaspoon dried oregano
1 cup shredded mozzarella cheese

Preparation:

1. In a 4-cup round baking dish that fits into your appliance, pour ¼ cup pasta sauce on the bottom of the dish. Place ¼ of the ground beef on top of the sauce. 2. In a small bowl, mix ricotta, Parmesan, garlic powder, parsley, and oregano. Place dollops of half the mixture on top of the beef. 3. Sprinkle with ⅓ of the mozzarella. Repeat layers until all beef, ricotta mixture, sauce, and mozzarella are used, ending with the mozzarella on top. 4. Cover dish with foil. Position the wire rack in the top rack height position and place the baking dish on the wire rack. Close the oven door and turn the FUNCTION dial until the indicator on the LCD screen points to BROIL. 5. Set the temperature to 370°F(190°C) with convection turned on and set the timer to 15 minutes. Press the START/CANCEL button to activate. 6. In the last 2 minutes of cooking, remove the foil to brown the cheese. 7. When cooking is complete, serve immediately.
Per Serving: Calories 389; Fat 19.08g; Sodium 433mg; Carbs 7.08g; Fiber 1.5g; Sugar 3.17g; Protein 45.18g

Easy Barbecued Meatballs

⏲ Prep: 10 minutes   🍲 Cook: 14 minutes   🍲 Serves: 4

Ingredients:

1 pound 80/20 ground beef
¼ pound ground Italian sausage
1 large egg
¼ teaspoon onion powder
½ teaspoon garlic powder
1 teaspoon dried parsley
4 slices sugar-free bacon, cooked and chopped
¼ cup chopped white onion
¼ cup chopped pickled jalapeños
½ cup low-carb, sugar-free barbecue sauce

Preparation:

1. In a large bowl, mix ground beef, sausage, and egg until fully combined. Mix in all remaining ingredients except barbecue sauce. Form into eight meatballs. Place meatballs on the baking pan. 2. Position the wire rack in the top rack height position and place the baking pan on the wire rack. Close the oven door and turn the FUNCTION dial until the indicator on the LCD screen points to BROIL. 3. Set the temperature to 400°F(205°C) with convection turned on and set the timer to 14 minutes. Press the START/CANCEL button to activate. 4. Turn the meatballs halfway through the cooking time. 5. When done, meatballs should be browned on the outside and have an internal temperature of at least 180°F. 6. Remove meatballs from oven and toss in barbecue sauce. Serve warm.
Per Serving: Calories 446; Fat 23.32g; Sodium 875mg; Carbs 16.43g; Fiber 0.6g; Sugar 12.52g; Protein 40.17g

Marinated Steak with Mushrooms

⏰ Prep: 10 minutes   🍴 Cook: 10 minutes   🍃 Serves: 4

) Ingredients:

1½ pounds sirloin, trimmed and cut into 1-inch strips
8 ounces brown mushrooms, halved
¼ cup Worcestershire sauce
1 tablespoon Dijon mustard
1 tablespoon olive oil
1 teaspoon paprika
1 teaspoon crushed red pepper flakes
2 tablespoons chopped fresh parsley (optional)

) Preparation:

1. Place the beef and mushrooms in a gallon-size resealable bag.
2. In a small bowl, whisk together the Worcestershire, mustard, paprika, olive oil, and red pepper flakes. Pour the marinade into the bag and massage gently to ensure the beef and mushrooms are evenly coated. 3. Seal the bag and refrigerate for at least 4 hours, preferably overnight. Remove from the refrigerator 30 minutes before starting to cook. 4. Drain and discard the marinade. Arrange the steak and mushrooms on the baking pan. 5. Position the wire rack in the top rack height position and place the baking pan on the wire rack. Close the oven door and turn the FUNCTION dial until the indicator on the LCD screen points to BROIL. 6. Set the temperature to 400°F(205°C) with convection turned on and set the timer to 10 minutes. Press the START/CANCEL button to activate. Pause through the cooking time to shake the pan. 7. When cooking is complete, transfer to a serving plate and top with the parsley, if desired.

Per Serving: Calories 248; Fat 8.06g; Sodium 353mg; Carbs 6.49g; Fiber 0.8g; Sugar 2.84g; Protein 36.07g

Simple Thai Beef Satay with Peanut Sauce

⏰ Prep: 10 minutes   🍴 Cook: 5 minutes   🍃 Serves: 4

) Ingredients:

Juice of 3 limes
½ cup fresh cilantro
4 cloves garlic
1-inch piece fresh ginger, peeled and chopped
2 tablespoons Swerve sugar replacement
2 tablespoons fish sauce
2 tablespoons reduced-sodium soy sauce
1 teaspoon sriracha or chili-garlic sauce
2 teaspoons sesame oil
1½ pounds flank steak, sliced ¼ inch thick against the grain
2 medium cucumbers, peeled and sliced
Peanut Sauce:
½ cup creamy peanut butter
Juice of ½ lime
1 tablespoon reduced-sodium soy sauce
1 teaspoon Swerve sugar replacement
1 teaspoon grated fresh ginger
1 teaspoon chili-garlic sauce
⅓ cup water

) Preparation:

1. In a food processor or blender, process the lime juice, garlic, cilantro, ginger, Swerve, fish sauce, sriracha, soy sauce, and sesame oil. 2. Place the steak slices into a gallon-size resealable bag and pour the marinade over the top of the meat. Seal the bag and refrigerate for at least an hour or up to 4 hours. 3. To make the peanut sauce by combining the peanut butter, Swerve, ginger, lime juice, soy sauce, and chili-garlic sauce in a medium bowl. Slowly add the water and whisk until smooth. Cover and refrigerate until ready to serve. 4. Discard the marinade and thread the meat slices back and forth onto skewers. Working in batches if necessary, place the satay skewers on the baking pan. 5. Position the wire rack in the bottom rack height position and close the oven door. Turn the FUNCTION dial until the indicator on the LCD screen points to the ROAST function. 6. Set the temperature to 400°F(205°C) with convection turned on and set the timer to 3 minutes. Press the START/CANCEL button to activate. 7. When preheating has completed, place the baking pan on the wire rack and roast for 2 or 3 minutes until cooked through, pausing halfway through the time to turn the skewers. 8. When cooking is complete, serve with the peanut sauce and the cucumbers.

Per Serving: Calories 495; Fat 23.25g; Sodium 1392mg; Carbs 25.19g; Fiber 3g; Sugar 10.43g; Protein 48.23g

Garlic London Broil with Herb Butter

⏱ Prep: 10 minutes   🍴 Cook: 25 minutes   🥬 Serves: 4

▶ Ingredients:

1½ pounds London broil top round steak
¼ cup olive oil
2 tablespoons balsamic vinegar
1 tablespoon Worcestershire sauce
4 cloves garlic, minced
Herb Butter:
6 tablespoons unsalted butter, softened
1 tablespoon chopped fresh parsley
¼ teaspoon salt
¼ teaspoon dried ground rosemary or thyme
¼ teaspoon garlic powder
Pinch of red pepper flakes

▶ Preparation:

1. Place the beef in a gallon-size resealable bag. In a small bowl, whisk together the Worcestershire sauce, olive oil, balsamic vinegar, and garlic. Pour the marinade over the beef, massaging gently to coat, and seal the bag. Let sit at room temperature for an hour or refrigerate overnight. 2. To make the herb butter by adding the butter, parsley, salt, garlic powder, rosemary, and red pepper flakes in a small bowl and mix until smooth. Cover and refrigerate until ready to use. 3. Remove the beef from the marinade, discard the marinade, and place the beef on the baking pan. 4. Position the wire rack in the bottom rack height position and close the oven door. Turn the FUNCTION dial until the indicator on the LCD screen points to the ROAST function. 5. Set the temperature to 400°F(205°C) with convection turned on and set the timer to 25 minutes. Press the START/CANCEL button to activate. 6. When preheating has completed, place the baking pan on the wire rack and roast for 20 to 25 minutes, until a thermometer inserted into the thickest part indicates the desired doneness, 125°F (rare) to 150°F (medium). Pause halfway through the cooking time to turn the meat. 7. When cooking is complete, let the beef rest for 10 minutes before slicing. Serve topped with the herb butter.
Per Serving: Calories 524; Fat 38.19g; Sodium 306mg; Carbs 4.5g; Fiber 0.3g; Sugar 2.24g; Protein 38.94g

Perfect Greek Meatballs with Tzatziki Sauce

⏱ Prep: 10 minutes   🍴 Cook: 15 minutes   🥬 Serves: 4

▶ Ingredients:

1 pound 85% lean ground beef
1 cup grated zucchini
½ cup crumbled feta cheese
2 tablespoons finely minced red onion
1 teaspoon garlic powder
1 teaspoon dried oregano
1 teaspoon salt
½ teaspoon freshly ground black pepper
2 teaspoons fresh lemon juice
Tzatziki sauce:
½ cup sour cream
¼ cup grated cucumber
1 tablespoon fresh lemon juice
½ teaspoon garlic powder
½ teaspoon dried dill
½ teaspoon salt
½ teaspoon freshly ground black pepper

▶ Preparation:

1. In a large mixing bowl, combine the beef, red onion, garlic powder, oregano, salt, zucchini, feta, black pepper, and lemon juice. Mix gently until thoroughly combined. Shape the mixture into 1¼-inch meatballs. 2. Working in batches if necessary, arrange the meatballs in a single layer on the baking pan and coat lightly with olive oil spray. 3. Position the wire rack in the bottom rack height position and close the oven door. Turn the FUNCTION dial until the indicator on the LCD screen points to the ROAST function. 4. Set the temperature to 350°F(175°C) with convection turned on and set the timer to 15 minutes. Press the START/CANCEL button to activate. 5. When preheating has completed, place the baking pan on the wire rack and cook for 10 to 15 minutes, until the meatballs are browned and a thermometer inserted into the center of a meatball registers 160°F. Pause halfway through the cooking time to shake the pan. 6. To make the tzatziki sauce by combining the sour cream, cucumber, lemon juice, dill, salt, garlic powder, and black pepper in a bowl. Stir until thoroughly combined. Serve with the meatballs.
Per Serving: Calories 345; Fat 24.17g; Sodium 1144mg; Carbs 5.62g; Fiber 0.6g; Sugar 1.35g; Protein 25.29g

Crispy Beef Fried Steak with Cream Gravy

⏱ Prep: 10 minutes   🍖 Cook: 10 minutes   ❧ Serves: 4

Ingredients:

4 small thin cube steaks (about 1 pound)
½ teaspoon salt
½ teaspoon freshly ground black pepper
¼ teaspoon garlic powder
1 egg, lightly beaten
1 cup crushed pork rinds (about 3 ounces)
Cream Gravy:
½ cup heavy cream
2 ounces cream cheese
¼ cup bacon grease
2–3 tablespoons water
2–3 dashes Worcestershire sauce
Salt and freshly ground black pepper

Preparation:

1. Working one at a time, place the steak between two sheets of parchment paper and use a meat mallet to pound to an even thickness. 2. In a small bowl, combine the pepper, salt, and garlic power. Season both sides of each steak with the mixture. 3. Place the egg in a small shallow dish and the pork rinds in another small shallow dish. Dip each steak first in the egg wash, followed by the pork rinds, pressing lightly to form an even coating. Working in batches if necessary, arrange the steaks in a single layer on the baking pan. 4. Position the wire rack in the bottom rack height position and close the oven door. Turn the FUNCTION dial until the indicator on the LCD screen points to the ROAST function. 5. Set the temperature to 400°F(205°C) with convection turned on and set the timer to 10 minutes. Press the START/CANCEL button to activate. 6. When preheating has completed, place the baking pan on the wire rack and cook for 10 minutes until crispy and cooked through. 7. To make the cream gravy by warming the cream, cream cheese, and bacon grease in a heavy-bottomed pot over medium heat, whisking until smooth. Reduce the heat if the mixture begins to boil. Continue whisking as you slowly add the water, 1 tablespoon at a time, until the sauce reaches the desired consistency. Season with the Worcestershire sauce and pepper and salt to taste. Serve over the chicken fried steaks.

Per Serving: Calories 444; Fat 32.68g; Sodium 787mg; Carbs 1.86g; Fiber 0.2g; Sugar 1.04g; Protein 35.49g

Delicious Chinese-Style Spareribs

⏱ Prep: 10 minutes   🍖 Cook: 35 minutes   ❧ Serves: 4

Ingredients:

1 tablespoon sesame oil
1 tablespoon fermented black bean paste
1 tablespoon seasoned rice vinegar
1 tablespoon reduced-sodium soy sauce
1 tablespoon Swerve sugar replacement
1 teaspoon minced garlic
1 teaspoon grated fresh ginger
2 pounds pork spareribs, cut into small pieces

Preparation:

1. In a small bowl, combine the sesame oil, rice vinegar, soy sauce, Swerve, garlic, black bean paste, and ginger. Stir until thoroughly combined. Transfer the marinade to a gallon-size resealable bag and add the ribs. Seal the bag and massage the ribs to coat with the marinade. Refrigerate for at least 4 hours, preferably overnight. 2. Working in batches if necessary, place the ribs in a single layer on the baking pan. 3. Position the wire rack in the bottom rack height position and close the oven door. Turn the FUNCTION dial until the indicator on the LCD screen points to the ROAST function. 4. Set the temperature to 380°F(195°C) with convection turned on and set the timer to 35 minutes. Press the START/CANCEL button to activate. 5. When preheating has completed, place the baking pan on the wire rack and roast for 30 to 35 minutes, until tender and browned. Pause halfway through the cooking time to turn the ribs. 6. When cooking is complete, garnish with scallions bend serve.

Per Serving: Calories 455; Fat 38.42g; Sodium 233mg; Carbs 3.39g; Fiber 0.1g; Sugar 2.57g; Protein 24.17g

Herbed Garlic Flank Steak

⏱ Prep: 5 minutes   🍲 Cook: 10 minutes   🥬 Serves: 6

Ingredients:

½ cup avocado oil
¼ cup coconut aminos
1 shallot, minced
1 tablespoon minced garlic
2 tablespoons chopped fresh oregano, or 2 teaspoons dried
1½ teaspoons sea salt
1 teaspoon freshly ground black pepper
¼ teaspoon red pepper flakes
2 pounds flank steak

Preparation:

1. In a blender, combine the avocado oil, coconut aminos, shallot, garlic, salt, oregano, black pepper, and red pepper flakes. Process until smooth. 2. Place the steak in a zip-top plastic bag or shallow dish with the marinade. Seal the bag or cover the dish and marinate in the refrigerator for at least 2 hours or overnight. 3. Remove the steak from the bag and discard the marinade. 4. Place the steak on the baking pan, if needed, cutting into sections and working in batches. 5. Position the wire rack in the bottom rack height position and close the oven door. Turn the FUNCTION dial until the indicator on the LCD screen points to the ROAST function. 6. Set the temperature to 380°F(195°C) with convection turned on and set the timer to 6 minutes. Press the START/CANCEL button to activate.

7. When preheating has completed, place the baking pan on the wire rack and roast for 4 to 6 minutes. Then flip the steak and cook for another 4 minutes or until the internal temperature reaches 120°F in the thickest part for medium-rare. 8. When cooking is complete, serve and enjoy.

Per Serving: Calories 418; Fat 27.78g; Sodium 667mg; Carbs 7.96g; Fiber 0.4g; Sugar 6.61g; Protein 32.79g

Low-Carb Spaghetti Zoodles and Meatballs

⏱ Prep: 15 minutes   🍲 Cook: 13 minutes   🥬 Serves: 6

Ingredients:

1 pound ground beef
1½ teaspoons sea salt, plus more for seasoning
1 large egg, beaten
1 teaspoon gelatin
¾ cup Parmesan cheese
2 teaspoons minced garlic
1 teaspoon Italian seasoning
Freshly ground black pepper
Avocado oil spray
Keto-friendly marinara sauce, such as Rao's Homemade®, for serving
6 ounces zucchini noodles, made using a spiralizer or store-bought

Preparation:

1. Place the ground beef in a large bowl and season with the salt. 2. Place the egg in a separate bowl and sprinkle with the gelatin. Allow to sit for 5 minutes. 3. Stir the gelatin mixture, then pour it over the ground beef. Add the Parmesan, garlic, and Italian seasoning. Season with pepper and salt. 4. Form the mixture into 1½-inch meatballs and place them on a plate. Then cover with plastic wrap and refrigerate for at least 1 hour or overnight. 5. Spray the meatballs with oil. Arrange the meatballs in a single layer on the baking pan. 6. Position the wire rack in the bottom rack height position and close the oven door. Turn the FUNCTION dial until the indicator on the LCD screen points to the ROAST function. 7. Set the temperature to 400°F(205°C) with convection turned on and set the timer to 4 minutes. Press the START/ CANCEL button to activate. 8. When preheating has completed, place the baking pan on the wire rack and roast for 4 minutes. Flip the meatballs and spray them with more oil. Cook for 4 minutes more, until an instant-read thermometer reads 160°F. Transfer the meatballs to a plate and allow them to rest. 9. While the meatballs are resting, heat the marinara in a saucepan on the stove over medium heat. 10. Place the zucchini noodles in the baking pan, place the baking pan on the wire rack, and with the BROIL function, cook at 400°F(205°C) for 3 to 5 minutes. 11. To serve, place the zucchini noodles in serving bowls. Top with meatballs and warm marinara.

Per Serving: Calories 176; Fat 8.44g; Sodium 907mg; Carbs 3.54g; Fiber 0.4g; Sugar 0.23g; Protein 21.79g

Hearty Cheeseburger Casserole

⏰ **Prep: 10 minutes**   🍲 **Cook: 70 minutes**   ❧ **Serves: 4**

Ingredients:

¼ pound reduced-sodium bacon
1 pound 85% lean ground beef
1 clove garlic, minced
¼ teaspoon onion powder
4 eggs
¼ cup heavy cream
¼ cup tomato paste
2 tablespoons dill pickle relish
¼ teaspoon salt
¼ teaspoon freshly ground black pepper
1½ cups grated Cheddar cheese, divided

Preparation:

1. Lightly coat a 6-cup casserole dish that will fit in oven, such an 8-inch round pan, with olive oil and set aside. 2. Place the bacon in a single layer on the baking pan. Position the wire rack in the top rack height position and place the baking pan on the wire rack. Close the oven door and turn the FUNCTION dial until the indicator on the LCD screen points to BROIL. 3. Set the temperature to 350°F(175°C) with convection turned on and set the timer to 10 minutes. Press the START/CANCEL button to activate. 4. Check for crispiness and cook for 2 to 3 minutes longer if needed. When cooking is complete, place the bacon on a plate lined with paper towels and let cool. Drain the grease. 5. Crumble the beef into a single layer on the baking pan. Scatter the garlic on top and sprinkle with the onion powder. Place the baking pan in the oven and cook at 350°F(175°C) for 15 to 20 minutes until the beef is browned and cooked through. 6. While the beef is cooking, in a bowl whisk together the eggs, tomato paste, pickle relish, salt, cream, and pepper. Stir in 1 cup of the cheese. Set aside. 7. When the beef is done, transfer it to the prepared 8-inch round pan. Use the side of a spoon to break up any large pieces of beef and drain the grease. 8. Crumble the bacon and add it to the beef, spreading the meats into an even layer. Pour the egg mixture over the beef mixture and top with the remaining ½ cup of cheese. 9. Place the prepared pan on the wire rack and, with the same function, cook at 350°F(175°C) for 20 to 25 minutes until the eggs are set and the top is golden brown. 10. When cooking is complete, serve and enjoy.

Per Serving: Calories 571; Fat 40.58g; Sodium 803mg; Carbs 5.93g; Fiber 0.5g; Sugar 3.7g; Protein 45.78g

Healthy Steak Salad with Smoky Blue Cheese Dressing

⏰ **Prep: 10 minutes**   🍲 **Cook: 15 minutes**   🍂 **Serves: 4**

Ingredients:

1 pound sirloin steak
1 tablespoon steak seasoning
8 cups chopped romaine lettuce
2 avocados, peeled, pitted, and sliced
½ cup cherry tomatoes, halved
¼ red onion, thinly sliced
¼ cup crumbled blue cheese
Smoky Blue Cheese Dressing:
½ cup mayonnaise
¼ cup buttermilk
1 tablespoon chipotle hot sauce
1 teaspoon garlic powder
½ teaspoon Worcestershire sauce
¼ cup crumbled blue cheese
Salt and freshly ground black pepper

Preparation:

1. Rub the steak with the steak seasoning. Arrange the steak on the baking pan and spray lightly with olive oil. 2. Position the wire rack in the bottom rack height position and close the oven door. Turn the FUNCTION dial until the indicator on the LCD screen points to the ROAST function. 3. Set the temperature to 400°F(205°C) with convection turned on and set the timer to 15 minutes. Press the START/CANCEL button to activate. 4. Pause halfway through the cooking time to turn the meat and cook until a thermometer inserted into the thickest part indicates the desired doneness, 125°F (rare) or 150°F (medium). 5. When cooking is complete, let the steaks rest for 10 minutes before slicing into bite-size pieces. 6. Meanwhile, to make the dressing by combining the mayonnaise, buttermilk, garlic powder, hot sauce, and Worcestershire sauce in a bow. Whisk until smooth. Stir in the blue cheese and season with freshly ground black pepper and salt. 7. To assemble the salad, place the lettuce on the bottom of the plate or serving bowl. Top with the avocado slices, tomatoes, and red onion, followed by the steak slices. Scatter the blue cheese crumbles on top and serve with the dressing on the side.

Per Serving: Calories 456; Fat 28.4g; Sodium 1289mg; Carbs 22.7g; Fiber 9.6g; Sugar 6.69g; Protein 30.78g

Chapter 7 Desserts Recipes

Vanilla Peanut Butter Cookies

⏱ **Prep: 5 minutes**   🍲 **Cook: 8 minutes**   🍃 **Serves: 8**

Ingredients:

1 cup no-sugar-added smooth peanut butter
⅓ cup granular erythritol
1 large egg
1 teaspoon vanilla extract

Preparation:

1. In a large bowl, mix all ingredients until smooth. Continue stirring for 2 additional minutes, and the mixture will begin to thicken. 2. Roll the mixture into eight balls and press gently down to flatten into 2" round disks. 3. Cut a piece of parchment to fit the baking pan and place it into the baking pan. Place the cookies onto the parchment, working in batches as necessary. 4. Position the rack in the middle rack height position. Turn the FUNCTION dial until the indicator on the LCD screen points to the COOKIES function. 5. Set the temperature to 320°F(160°C) and the timer to 8 minutes. Press the START/CANCEL button to activate. 5. When preheating has completed, place the baking pan on the wire rack and bake. 6. Flip the cookies at the 6-minute mark. 7. When cooking is complete, serve completely cooled.
Per Serving: Calories 226; Fat 14.73g; Sodium 362mg; Carbs 13.37g; Fiber 1.9g; Sugar 3.43g; Protein 12.71g

Chocolate Chip Cookies

⏱ **Prep: 10 minutes**   🍲 **Cook: 10 minutes**   🍃 **Serves: 6**

Ingredients:

2 cups almond flour
¼ cup Swerve sugar replacement
Scant ½ teaspoon salt
¼ teaspoon baking soda
½ cup sugar-free chocolate chips
½ cup chopped pecans
¼ cup coconut oil
1 teaspoon vanilla extract
2 tablespoons milk, as needed

Preparation:

1. Line the baking pan with parchment paper. 2. In a large bowl, combine the almond flour, Swerve, salt, chocolate chips, baking soda, and pecans. Add the coconut oil and vanilla extract and stir until thoroughly combined. Add the milk, a teaspoon or two at a time as needed, until the mixture forms a stiff dough. 3. Roll the dough into 12 equal-size balls. Flatten slightly to form cookie-shaped disks. Arrange the cookies in the baking pan, in batches if necessary, so they don't touch. 4. Position the rack in the middle rack height position. Turn the FUNCTION dial until the indicator on the LCD screen points to the COOKIES function. 5. Set the temperature to 300°F(150°C) and the timer to 10 minutes. Press the START/

CANCEL button to activate. 6. When preheating has completed, place the baking pan on the wire rack and bake for 8 to 10 minutes until the cookies begin to brown. 7. When cooking is complete, cool completely before removing from the oven and the cookies will harden as they cool.
Per Serving: Calories 329; Fat 16.56g; Sodium 269mg; Carbs 40.26g; Fiber 2g; Sugar 6.15g; Protein 5.44g

Perfect Chocolate Mayo Cake

⏰ Prep: 10 minutes   🍲 Cook: 25 minutes   🍃 Serves: 6

Ingredients:

1 cup blanched finely ground almond flour
¼ cup salted butter, melted
½ cup plus 1 tablespoon granular erythritol
1 teaspoon vanilla extract
¼ cup full-fat mayonnaise
¼ cup unsweetened cocoa powder
2 large eggs

Preparation:

1. In a large bowl, mix all ingredients until smooth. 2. Pour batter into a 6" round baking pan that fits into your appliance. 3. Position the wire rack in the bottom rack height position and close the oven door. Turn the FUNCTION dial until the indicator on the LCD screen points to the BAKE function. 3. Set the temperature to 300°F(150°C) with convection turned on and set the timer to 25 minutes. Press the START/CANCEL button to activate. 4. When preheating has completed, place the baking pan on the wire rack and bake. 5. When done, a toothpick inserted in center will come out clean. Allow cake to cool completely, or it will crumble when moved.
Per Serving: Calories 233; Fat 12.98g; Sodium 397mg; Carbs 20.55g; Fiber 1.6g; Sugar 0.67g; Protein 10.22g

Sweet Cream Puffs

⏰ Prep: 15 minutes   🍲 Cook: 6 minutes   🍃 Serves: 8

Ingredients:

½ cup blanched finely ground almond flour
½ cup low-carb vanilla protein powder
½ cup granular erythritol
½ teaspoon baking powder
1 large egg
5 tablespoons unsalted butter, melted
2 ounces full-fat cream cheese
¼ cup powdered erythritol
¼ teaspoon ground cinnamon
2 tablespoons heavy whipping cream
½ teaspoon vanilla extract

Preparation:

1. Mix almond flour, protein powder, baking powder, granular erythritol, egg, and butter in a large bowl until a soft dough forms. 2. Place the dough in the freezer for 20 minutes. Wet your hands with water and roll the dough into eight balls. 3. Cut a piece of parchment to fit the baking pan. Working in batches as necessary, place the dough balls into the baking pan on top of parchment. 4. Position the wire rack in the bottom rack height position and close the oven door. Turn the FUNCTION dial until the indicator on the LCD screen points to the BAKE function. 5. Set the temperature to 380°F(195°C) with convection turned on and set the timer to 6 minutes. Press the START/CANCEL button to activate. 6. When preheating has completed, place the baking pan on the wire rack and bake. 7. Flip cream puffs halfway through the cooking time. 8. When cooking is complete, remove the puffs and allow to cool. 8. In a medium bowl, beat the cream cheese, cinnamon, cream, powdered erythritol, and vanilla until fluffy. 9. Place the mixture into a pastry bag or a storage bag with the end snipped. Cut a small hole in the bottom of each puff and fill with some of the cream mixture. 10. Store in an airtight container up to 2 days in the refrigerator.
Per Serving: Calories 203; Fat 13.07g; Sodium 316mg; Carbs 11.18g; Fiber 1.8g; Sugar 1.27g; Protein 11.97g

Crispy Peanut Butter Cookies

⏱ **Prep:** 5 minutes   🍽 **Cook:** 15 minutes   ❧ **Serves:** 6

Ingredients:

½ cup peanut butter
½ cup Swerve sugar replacement
1 egg

Preparation:

1. Line the baking pan with parchment paper. 2. In a stand mixer fitted with a paddle attachment, beat the peanut butter and Swerve until fluffy. Beat in the egg. 3. Working in batches, roll a spoonful of dough into a ball, arrange in the baking pan, leaving enough space between the cookies so they don't touch when flattened, and use the back of a fork to flatten the cookies and make the traditional crisscross pattern. 4. Position the rack in the middle rack height position. Turn the FUNCTION dial until the indicator on the LCD screen points to the COOKIES function. 5. Set the temperature to 350°F (175°C) and the timer to 15 minutes. Press the START/CANCEL button to activate. 6. When preheating has completed, place the baking pan on the wire rack and bake for 12 to 15 minutes until the edges are lightly golden. 7. When cooking is complete, cool completely before removing from the oven and the cookies will harden as they cool.
Per Serving: Calories 168; Fat 8.86g; Sodium 140mg; Carbs 16.92g; Fiber 1.2g; Sugar 10.41g; Protein 7.14g

Yummy Double Chocolate Brownies

⏱ **Prep:** 5 minutes   🍽 **Cook:** 20 minutes   ❧ **Serves:** 8

Ingredients:

1 cup almond flour
½ cup unsweetened cocoa powder
½ teaspoon baking powder
⅓ cup Swerve sugar replacement
¼ teaspoon salt
½ cup unsalted butter, melted and cooled
3 eggs
1 teaspoon vanilla extract
2 tablespoons mini semisweet chocolate chips

Preparation:

1. Line an 8-inch cake pan that fits into your appliance with parchment paper and brush with vegetable oil. 2. In a large bowl, combine the almond flour, baking powder, Swerve, cocoa powder, and salt. Add the butter, eggs, and vanilla. Stir until thoroughly combined. Arrange the batter into the prepared pan and scatter the chocolate chips on top. 3. Position the wire rack in the bottom rack height position and close the oven door. Turn the FUNCTION dial until the indicator on the LCD screen points to the BAKE function. 4. Set the temperature to 350°F(175°C) with convection turned on and set the timer to 20 minutes. Press the START/CANCEL button to activate. 5. When preheating has completed, place the pan on the wire rack and bake for 15 to 20 minutes until the edges are set and the center should still appear slightly undercooked. 6. When cooking is complete, let cool completely before slicing. To store, cover and refrigerate the brownies for up to 3 days.
Per Serving: Calories 198; Fat 11.06g; Sodium 103mg; Carbs 21.81g; Fiber 2.3g; Sugar 6.16g; Protein 5.28g

Cinnamon Cupcakes with Cream Cheese Frosting

⏰ **Prep: 5 minutes**   🍲 **Cook: 25 minutes**   🍃 **Serves: 6**

Ingredients:

½ cup plus 2 tablespoons almond flour
2 tablespoons low-carb vanilla protein powder
⅛ teaspoon salt
1 teaspoon baking powder
¼ teaspoon ground cinnamon
¼ cup unsalted butter
¼ cup Swerve sugar replacement
2 eggs
½ teaspoon vanilla extract
2 tablespoons heavy cream
Cream Cheese Frosting:
4 ounces cream cheese, softened
2 tablespoons unsalted butter, softened
½ teaspoon vanilla extract
2 tablespoons powdered Swerve sugar replacement
1–2 tablespoons heavy cream

Preparation:

1. Lightly coat 6 silicone muffin cups that fits into your appliance with vegetable oil and set aside. 2. In a medium bowl, combine the baking powder, almond flour, protein powder, salt, and cinnamon; set aside. 3. In a stand mixer fitted with a paddle attachment, beat the butter and Swerve until creamy. Add the eggs, vanilla, and heavy cream, and beat again until thoroughly combined. Add half the flour mixture at a time to the butter mixture, mixing after each addition, until you have a smooth, creamy batter. 4. Divide the batter evenly among the muffin cups, filling each one about three-fourths full. 5. Position the wire rack in the bottom rack height position and close the oven door. Turn the FUNCTION dial until the indicator on the LCD screen points to the BAKE function. 6. Set the temperature to 320°F(160°C) with convection turned on and set the timer to 25 minutes. Press the START/CANCEL button to activate. 7. When preheating has completed, place the muffin cups on the wire rack and bake for 20 to 25 minutes, or until a toothpick inserted into the center of a cupcake comes out clean. Transfer the cupcakes to a rack and let cool completely. 8. To make the cream cheese frosting: In a stand mixer fitted with a paddle attachment, beat the cream cheese, butter, and vanilla until fluffy. Add the Swerve and mix again until thoroughly combined. With the mixer running, add the heavy cream a tablespoon at a time until the frosting is smooth and creamy. Frost the cupcakes as desired.
Per Serving: Calories 252; Fat 18.19g; Sodium 188mg; Carbs 15.5g; Fiber 0.8g; Sugar 5.83g; Protein 6.72g

Rich Chocolate Cake

⏰ **Prep: 5 minutes**   🍲 **Cook: 9 minutes**   🍃 **Serves: 2**

Ingredients:

1 egg
2 tablespoons unsweetened cocoa powder
2 tablespoons water
2 tablespoons Swerve sugar replacement
1 tablespoon flaxseed meal
1 tablespoon vegetable oil
½ teaspoon baking powder
⅛ teaspoon vanilla extract
Pinch of salt
Sugar-free whipped topping (optional)

Preparation:

1. Coat a 2-cup baking dish or ramekin that fits into your appliance with vegetable oil and set aside. 2. In a small bowl, combine the egg, water, Swerve, flaxseed meal, cocoa powder, vegetable oil, baking powder, and vanilla. Stir until thoroughly combined. Transfer the mixture to the prepared baking dish. Sprinkle the top with a pinch of salt. 3. Position the wire rack in the bottom rack height position and close the oven door. Turn the FUNCTION dial until the indicator on the LCD screen points to the BAKE function. 4. Set the temperature to 350°F(175°C) with convection turned on and set the timer to 9 minutes. Press the START/CANCEL button to activate. 5. When preheating has completed, place the baking pan on the wire rack and bake for 8 to 9 minutes until the edges begin to firm. 6. Let the cake cool for a few minutes before taking it out of the oven. Serve warm with whipped topping, if desired.
Per Serving: Calories 163; Fat 11.78g; Sodium 326mg; Carbs 13.39g; Fiber 3g; Sugar 8.11g; Protein 4.68g

Cirtus Doughnut Bites

⏱ Prep: 5 minutes 🍲 Cook: 6 minutes 🍂 Serves: 10

Ingredients:

¾ cup water
8 tablespoons unsalted butter, divided
4 tablespoons Swerve sugar replacement, divided
½ teaspoon salt
¾ cup almond flour
⅓ cup coconut flour
1 teaspoon baking powder
Zest of 1 orange
2 eggs
1 teaspoon vanilla extract
2 teaspoons ground cinnamon

Preparation:

1. Line the baking pan with parchment paper and set aside. 2. In a medium pot over medium-high heat, combine the water, 5 tablespoons of the butter, 2 tablespoons of the Swerve, and the salt. Bring the mixture to boil, whisking until the butter is melted. Remove from the heat and let cool for a few minutes. 3. In a large mixing bowl, whisk together the almond flour, baking powder, coconut flour, and orange zest. Add the dry ingredients to the water mixture in the pot. Stir briskly. The mixture should be the consistency of loose mashed potatoes. 4. In a small bowl, whisk the eggs and vanilla. Add the egg mixture to the pot and whisk until smooth. Let sit for 10 to 15 minutes until the dough thickens. 5. Transfer the dough to a resealable bag. Cut a ¼-inch tip from one corner of the bag. Squeeze about 20 1½-inch mounds onto parchment paper. Freeze for 45 minutes or until hard. 6. Working in batches if necessary, place the doughnuts on the baking pan. 7. Position the wire rack in the bottom rack height position and close the oven door. Turn the FUNCTION dial until the indicator on the LCD screen points to the BAKE function. 8. Set the temperature to 400°F(205°C) with convection turned on and set the timer to 6 minutes. Press the START/CANCEL button to activate. 9. When preheating has completed, place the baking pan on the wire rack and bake for 6 minutes until brown and crisp. 10. In a small shallow bowl, combine the cinnamon and the remaining 2 tablespoons Swerve. In another small, shallow microwavable bowl, melt the remaining 3 tablespoons butter in the microwave on high for 30 seconds to 1 minute. While the doughnuts are warm, brush with the melted butter and roll in the cinnamon-Swerve mixture. Serve warm.

Per Serving: Calories 136; Fat 7.27g; Sodium 134mg; Carbs 14.98g; Fiber 0.8g; Sugar 4g; Protein 2.79g

Crispy Chocolate-Pecan Biscotti

⏱ Prep: 15 minutes 🍲 Cook: 22 minutes 🍂 Serves: 10

Ingredients:

1¼ cups finely ground blanched almond flour
¾ teaspoon baking powder
½ teaspoon xanthan gum
¼ teaspoon sea salt
3 tablespoons unsalted butter, at room temperature
⅓ cup Swerve Confectioners sweetener
1 large egg, beaten
1 teaspoon pure vanilla extract
⅓ cup chopped pecans
¼ cup stevia-sweetened chocolate chips, such as Lily's Sweets brand
Melted stevia-sweetened chocolate chips and chopped pecans, for topping (optional)

Preparation:

1. In a large bowl, combine the xanthan gum, almond flour, baking powder, and salt. 2. Line a 7-inch cake pan that fits inside your oven with parchment paper. 3. In the bowl of a stand mixer, beat the butter and Swerve. Add the beaten egg and vanilla, and beat for about 3 minutes. 4. Add the almond flour mixture to the butter-and-egg mixture and beat until just combined. 5. Stir in the pecans and chocolate chips. 6. Transfer the dough to the prepared pan, and press it into the bottom. 7. Position the rack in the middle rack height position. Turn the FUNCTION dial until the indicator on the LCD screen points to the COOKIES function. 8. Set the temperature to 325°F(165°C) and the timer to 12 minutes. Press the START/CANCEL button to activate. 9. When preheating has completed, place the pan on the wire rack and bake for 12 minutes. 10. Remove from the oven and let cool for 15 minutes. Using a sharp knife, cut the cookie into thin strips, then return the strips to the cake pan with the bottom sides facing up. 11. Cook at 300°F(150°C) for 8 to 10 minutes. 12. Remove from the oven and allow to cool completely on a wire rack. If desired, dredge one side of each biscotti piece into the melted chocolate chips, and top with the chopped pecans.

Per Serving: Calories 174; Fat 9.5g; Sodium 71mg; Carbs 19.6g; Fiber 1.3g; Sugar 5.73g; Protein 3.24g

Fluffy Almond Flour Cinnamon Rolls

⏰ Prep: 20 minutes   🍲 Cook: 18 minutes   🍽 Serves: 8

Ingredients:

3 tablespoons unsalted butter, at room temperature
½ cup brown sugar substitute, such as Sukrin Gold
1 teaspoon ground cinnamon
1½ cups finely ground blanched almond flour
¼ teaspoon sea salt
¼ teaspoon baking soda
¼ teaspoon xanthan gum
1 large egg, at room temperature
2 tablespoons unsalted butter, melted and cooled
1 tablespoon Swerve Confectioners sweetener
Avocado oil spray
Almond Glaze, for serving

Preparation:

1. In the bowl of a stand mixer, beat the butter, brown sugar substitute, and cinnamon. Set aside. 2. In a large bowl, combine the almond flour, salt, baking soda, and xanthan gum. 3. In a separate bowl, beat the egg. Stir in the cooled melted butter and Swerve until combined. 4. Add the egg-and-butter mixture to the flour mixture and knead with your clean hands until the dough is smooth. 5. Spray a large bowl with oil, add the dough, and coat it in the oil. Cover and refrigerate for 30 minutes. 6. Place the dough on a piece of parchment paper and form it into a rectangle. Put another piece of parchment on top of the dough and roll out the dough to a large rectangle, about ¼-inch thick. 7. Spread the butter and brown sugar mixture on top of the dough, and then roll up the dough from the long side. 8. Slice the rolled dough into 8 equal-size pieces, and arrange these in a parchment paper–lined 7-inch cake pan that fits inside your oven. 9. Position the rack in the middle rack height position. Turn the FUNCTION dial until the indicator on the LCD screen points to the COOKIES function. 10. Set the temperature to 300°F(150°C) and the timer to 18 minutes. Press the START/CANCEL button to activate. 11. When preheating has completed, place the baking pan on the wire rack and bake for 16 to 18 minutes, until the tops of the rolls are lightly browned. 12. When cooking is complete, let the rolls cool for 5 minutes, then invert them onto a plate. Sprinkle any cinnamon sugar mixture that has collected on the bottom of the pan over the top of the rolls. 13. Drizzle the Almond Glaze over the cinnamon rolls and serve warm.

Per Serving: Calories 151; Fat 5.86g; Sodium 135mg; Carbs 20.76g; Fiber 0.8g; Sugar 1.33g; Protein 3.57g

Sweet Chocolate Soufflés

⏰ Prep: 15 minutes   🍲 Cook: 14 minutes   🍽 Serves: 2

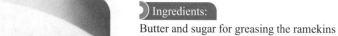

Ingredients:

Butter and sugar for greasing the ramekins
3 ounces semi-sweet chocolate, chopped
¼ cup unsalted butter
2 eggs, yolks and white separated
3 tablespoons sugar
½ teaspoon pure vanilla extract
2 tablespoons all-purpose flour
Powdered sugar, for dusting the finished soufflés
Heavy cream, for serving

Preparation:

1. Butter and sugar two 6-ounce ramekins. 2. In the microwave or a double boiler, melt the chocolate and butter together. In a separate bowl, whip the egg yolks vigorously. Add the sugar and the vanilla extract and beat well again. Drizzle in the chocolate and butter mixture, mixing well. Stir in the flour and combine until there are no lumps. 3. In a separate bowl, beat the egg whites to soft peak stage. Pour the whipped egg whites into the chocolate mixture gently and in stages. 4. Transfer the batter carefully to the buttered ramekins, leaving about ½-inch at the top. Place the ramekins on the baking pan. 5. Position the wire rack in the bottom rack height position and close the oven door. Turn the FUNCTION dial until the indicator on the LCD screen points to the BAKE function. 6. Set the temperature to 330(165°C) with convection turned on and set the timer to 14 minutes. Press the START/CANCEL button to activate. 7. When preheating has completed, place the baking pan on the wire rack and bake for 14 minutes. The soufflés should have risen nicely and be brown on top. 8. Dust with the powdered sugar and serve immediately with the heavy cream to pour over the top at the table.

Per Serving: Calories 552; Fat 39.68g; Sodium 85mg; Carbs 45.67g; Fiber 2.6g; Sugar 35.53g; Protein 9.18g

Crispy Caramel Apple Crumble

⏱ **Prep: 15 minutes**   🍲 **Cook: 50 minutes**   ❧ **Serves: 6-8**

Ingredients:

4 apples, peeled and thinly sliced
2 tablespoons sugar
1 tablespoon flour
1 teaspoon ground cinnamon
¼ teaspoon ground allspice
Healthy pinch ground nutmeg
10 caramel squares, cut into small pieces
Crumble topping:
¾ cup rolled oats
¼ cup sugar
⅓ cup flour
¼ teaspoon ground cinnamon
6 tablespoons butter, melted

Preparation:

1. Combine the apples, sugar, flour, and spices in a large bowl and toss to coat. Add the caramel pieces and mix well. Pour the apple mixture into a 1-quart round baking dish that will fit in your oven (6-inch diameter). 2. Make the crumble topping by combining the rolled oats, sugar, flour and cinnamon in a small bowl. Add the melted butter and mix well. Top the apples with the crumble mixture. Cover the entire dish with aluminum foil. 3. Position the wire rack in the bottom rack height position and close the oven door. Turn the FUNCTION dial until the indicator on the LCD screen points to the BAKE function. 4. Set the temperature to 330(165°C) with convection turned on and set the timer to 25 minutes. Press the START/CANCEL button to activate. 5. When preheating has completed, place the baking pan on the wire rack and bake. 6. Remove the aluminum foil and continue to bake for another 25 minutes. 7. When cooking is complete, serve the crumble warm with the whipped cream or vanilla ice cream, if desired.

Per Serving: Calories 352; Fat 14.53g; Sodium 44mg; Carbs 53.24g; Fiber 4g; Sugar 28.6g; Protein 5.36g

Yummy Molten Chocolate Almond Cakes

⏱ **Prep: 15 minutes**   🍲 **Cook: 13 minutes**   ❧ **Serves: 3**

Ingredients:

Butter and flour for the ramekins
4 ounces bittersweet chocolate, chopped
½ cup (1 stick) unsalted butter
2 eggs
2 egg yolks
¼ cup sugar
½ teaspoon pure vanilla extract, or almond extract
1 tablespoon all-purpose flour
3 tablespoons ground almonds
8 to 12 semisweet chocolate discs (or 4 chunks of chocolate)
Cocoa powder or powdered sugar, for dusting
Toasted almonds, coarsely chopped

Preparation:

1. Butter and flour three (6-ounce) ramekins. 2. In the microwave or a double boiler, melt the chocolate and butter together. In a separate bowl, whip the eggs, egg yolks and sugar together until light and smooth. Add the vanilla extract. Pour the chocolate mixture into the egg mixture and whisk. Stir in the flour and ground almonds. 3. Transfer the batter carefully to the buttered ramekins, filling halfway. Place two or three chocolate discs in the center of the batter and then fill the ramekins to ½-inch below the top with the remaining batter. Place the ramekins on the baking pan. 4. Position the wire rack in the bottom rack height position and close the oven door. Turn the FUNCTION dial until the indicator on the LCD screen points to the BAKE function. 5. Set the temperature to 330(165°C) with convection turned on and set the timer to 13 minutes. Press the START/CANCEL button to activate. 6. When preheating has completed, place the baking pan on the wire rack and bake. 7. The sides of the cake should be set, but the centers should be slightly soft. Remove the ramekins from the oven and let the cakes sit for 5 minutes. 8. Run a butter knife around the edge of the ramekins and invert the cakes onto a plate. Lift the ramekin off the plate slowly and carefully so that the cake doesn't break. Dust with cocoa powder or powdered sugar and serve with a scoop of ice cream and some coarsely chopped toasted almonds.

Per Serving: Calories 506; Fat 32.91g; Sodium 90mg; Carbs 46.23g; Fiber 2.2g; Sugar 36.01g; Protein 8.9g

Conclusion

The Breville Smart Oven Air Fryer Pro cookbook serves as a culinary companion, unlocking the full potential of this versatile kitchen appliance. With a diverse array of recipes spanning appetizers, mains, sides, and desserts, it caters to every palate and occasion. From crispy golden fries to succulent roasted meats, each dish is crafted with precision and innovation, showcasing the appliance's multifunctionality. With detailed instructions and insightful tips, even novice cooks can effortlessly create restaurant-quality meals. Whether you're cooking for a family dinner or entertaining guests, the cookbook empowers you to elevate your cooking game and embrace the art of home cooking with confidence and flair.

Appendix 1 Measurement Conversion Chart

WEIGHT EQUIVALENTS

US STANDARD	METRIC (APPROX-INATE)
1 ounce	28 g
2 ounces	57 g
5 ounces	142 g
10 ounces	284 g
15 ounces	425 g
16 ounces (1 pound)	455 g
1.5pounds	680 g
2pounds	907 g

TEMPERATURES EQUIVALENTS

FAHRENHEIT(F)	CELSIUS (C) (APPROXIMATE)
225 °F	107 °C
250 °F	120 °C
275 °F	135 °C
300 °F	150 °C
325 °F	160 °C
350 °F	180 °C
375 °F	190 °C
400 °F	205 °C
425 °F	220 °C
450 °F	235 °C
475 °F	245 °C
500 °F	260 °C

VOLUME EQUIVALENTS (DRY)

US STANDARD	METRIC (APPROXIMATE)
⅛ teaspoon	0.5 mL
¼ teaspoon	1 mL
½ teaspoon	2 mL
¾ teaspoon	4 mL
1 teaspoon	5 mL
1 tablespoon	15 mL
¼ cup	59 mL
½ cup	118 mL
¾ cup	177 mL
1 cup	235 mL
2 cups	475 mL
3 cups	700 mL
4 cups	1 L

VOLUME EQUIVALENTS (LIQUID)

US STANDARD	US STANDARD (OUNCES)	METRIC (APPROXIMATE)
2 tablespoons	1 fl.oz	30 mL
¼ cup	2 fl.oz	60 mL
½ cup	4 fl.oz	120 mL
1 cup	8 fl.oz	240 mL
1½ cup	12 fl.oz	355 mL
2 cups or 1 pint	16 fl.oz	475 mL
4 cups or 1 quart	32 fl.oz	1 L
1 gallon	128 fl.oz	4 L

Appendix 2 Air Fryer Cooking Chart

Vegetables	Temp (°F)	Time (min)
Asparagus	375	4 to 6
Baked Potatoes	400	35 to 45
Broccoli	400	8 to 10
Brussels Sprouts	350	15 to 18
Butternut Squash (cubed)	375	20 to 25
Carrots	375	15 to 25
Cauliflower	400	10 to 12
Corn on the Cob	390	6
Eggplant	400	15
Green Beans	375	16 to 20
Kale	250	12
Mushrooms	400	5
Peppers	375	8 to 10
Sweet Potatoes (whole)	380	30 to 35
Tomatoes (halved, sliced)	350	10
Zucchini (½-inch sticks)	400	12

Frozen Foods	Temp (°F)	Time (min)
Breaded Shrimp	400	9
Chicken Burger	360	11
Chicken Nudgets	400	10
Corn Dogs	400	7
Curly Fries (1 to 2 lbs.)	400	11 to 14
Fish Sticks (10 oz.)	400	10
French Fries	380	15 to 20
Hash Brown	360	15 to 18
Meatballs	380	6 to 8
Mozzarella Sticks	400	8
Onion Rings (8 oz.)	400	8
Pizza	390	5 to 10
Pot Pie	360	25
Pot Sticks (10 oz.)	400	8
Sausage Rolls	400	15
Spring Rolls	400	15 to 20

Meat and Seafood	Temp (°F)	Time (min)
Bacon	400	5 to 10
Beef Eye Round Roast (4 lbs.)	390	45 to 55
Bone to in Pork Chops	400	4 to 5 per side
Brats	400	8 to 10
Burgers	350	8 to 10
Chicken Breast	375	22 to 23
Chicken Tender	400	14 to 16
Chicken Thigh	400	25
Chicken Wings (2 lbs.)	400	10 to 12
Cod	370	8 to 10
Fillet Mignon (8 oz.)	400	14 to 18
Fish Fillet (0.5 lb., 1-inch)	400	10
Flank Steak(1.5 lbs.)	400	10 to 14
Lobster Tails (4 oz.)	380	5 to 7
Meatballs	400	7 to 10
Meat Loaf	325	35 to 45
Pork Chops	375	12 to 15
Salmon	400	5 to 7
Salmon Fillet (6 oz.)	380	12
Sausage Patties	400	8 to 10
Shrimp	375	8
Steak	400	7 to 14
Tilapia	400	8 to 12
Turkey Breast (3 lbs.)	360	40 to 50
Whole Chicken (6.5 lbs.)	360	75

Desserts	Temp (°F)	Time (min)
Apple Pie	320	30
Brownies	350	17
Churros	360	13
Cookies	350	5
Cupcakes	330	11
Doughnuts	360	5
Roasted Bananas	375	8
Peaches	350	5

Appendix 3 Recipes Index

Made in United States
Troutdale, OR
01/10/2025

27774243R00042